THE REAL LOW INCOME SAVINGS CHALLENGES
JUST $5 OR LESS PER DAY

Saving money has never been easier!

This book provides a variety of achievable savings challenges designed for beginners and low-income budgets. **The focus is on setting aside just $5 or less per day through short-term and long-term plans.** By following these simple, structured challenges, you can build a consistent savings habit and start securing your financial future, no matter your daily income level.

Suggestion: Colorize as you progress.

Hyperion Darby

Member of PageTitans

This book may not be copied, scanned, or distributed in any form, whether electronic or printed, without the prior written consent of the author.

Let's Save .... $55 in 30 Days

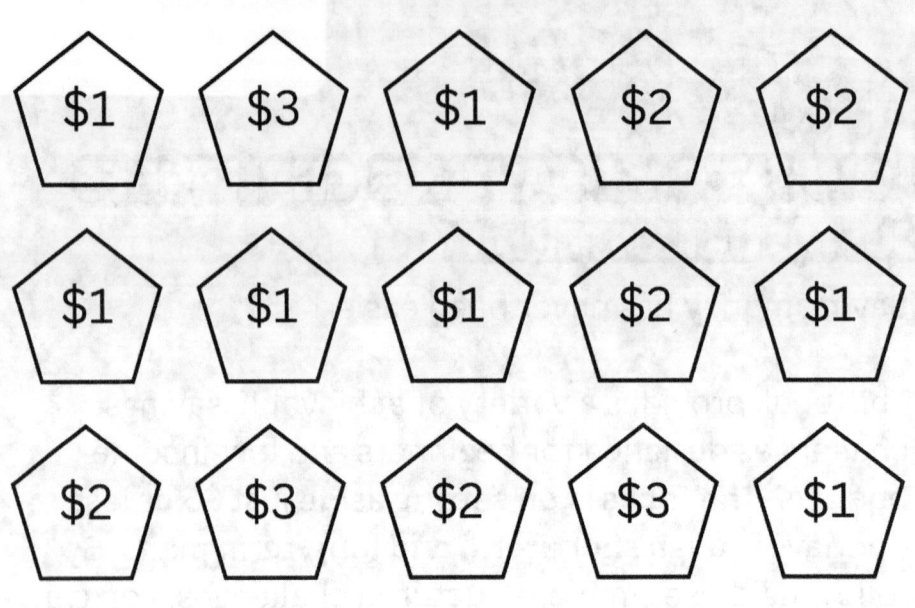

Save for Short-Term Goals: Save for short-term goals, such as a new toy or game.

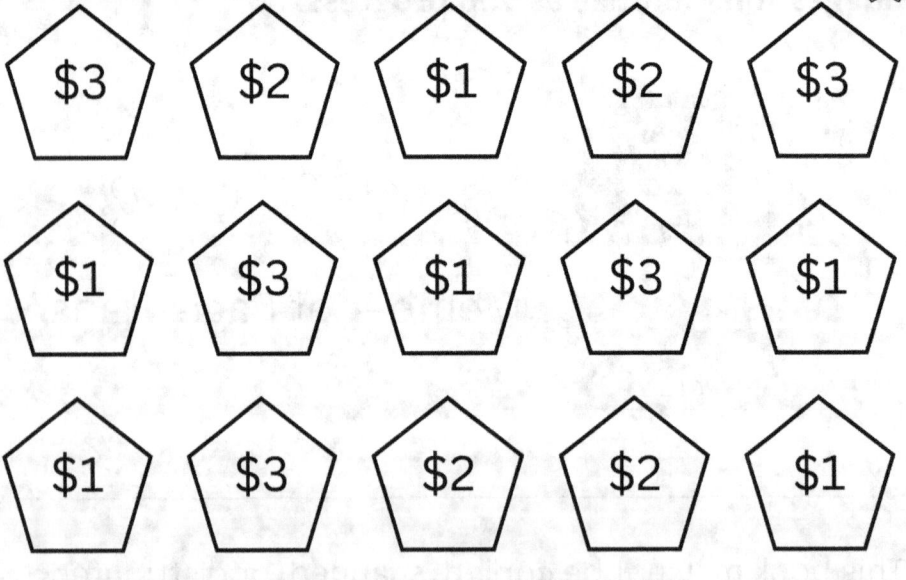

Notes: _____
_____

Let's Save .... $65 in 35 Days

Notes: _____

Let's Save .... $25 in 12 Days

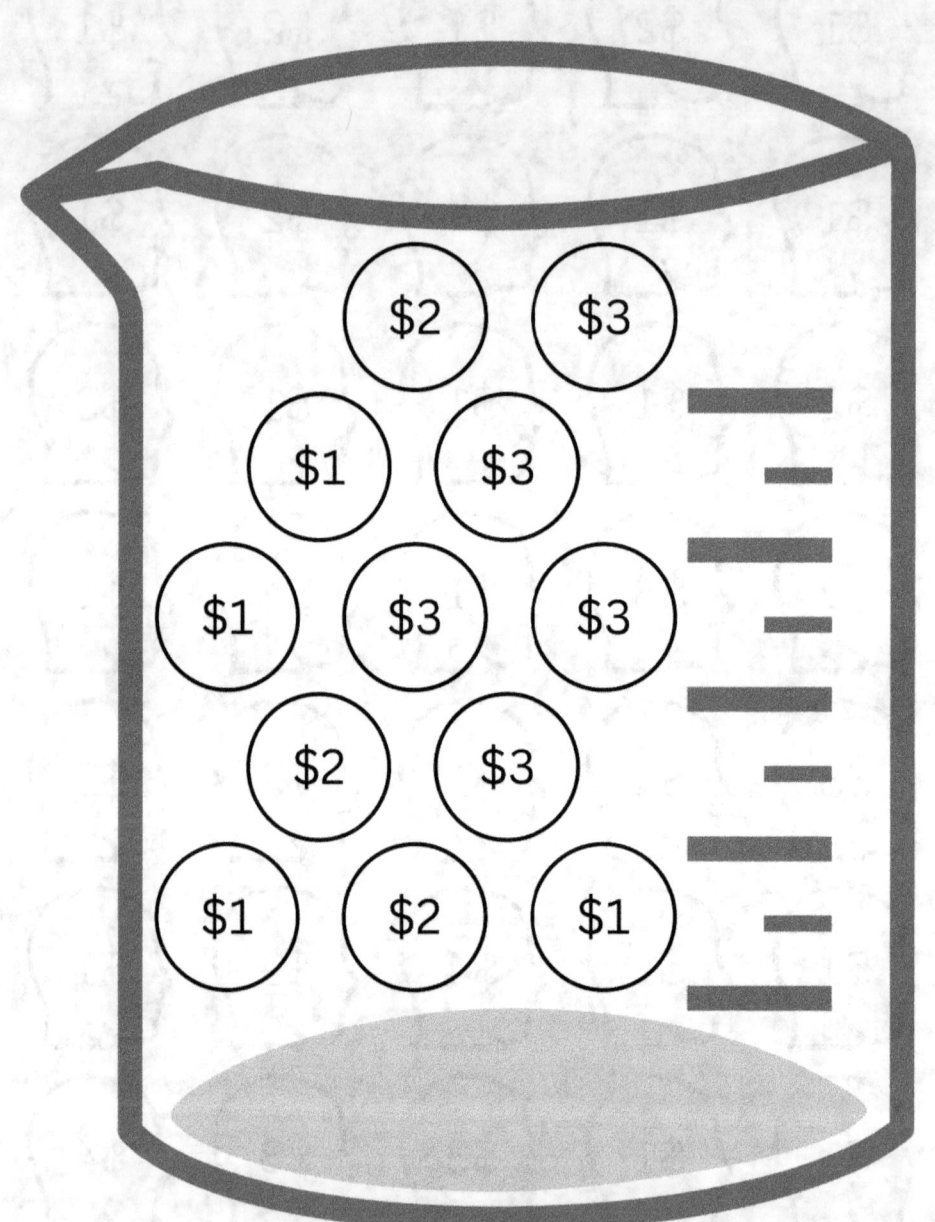

Notes: _____

Let's Save .... $85 in 30 Days

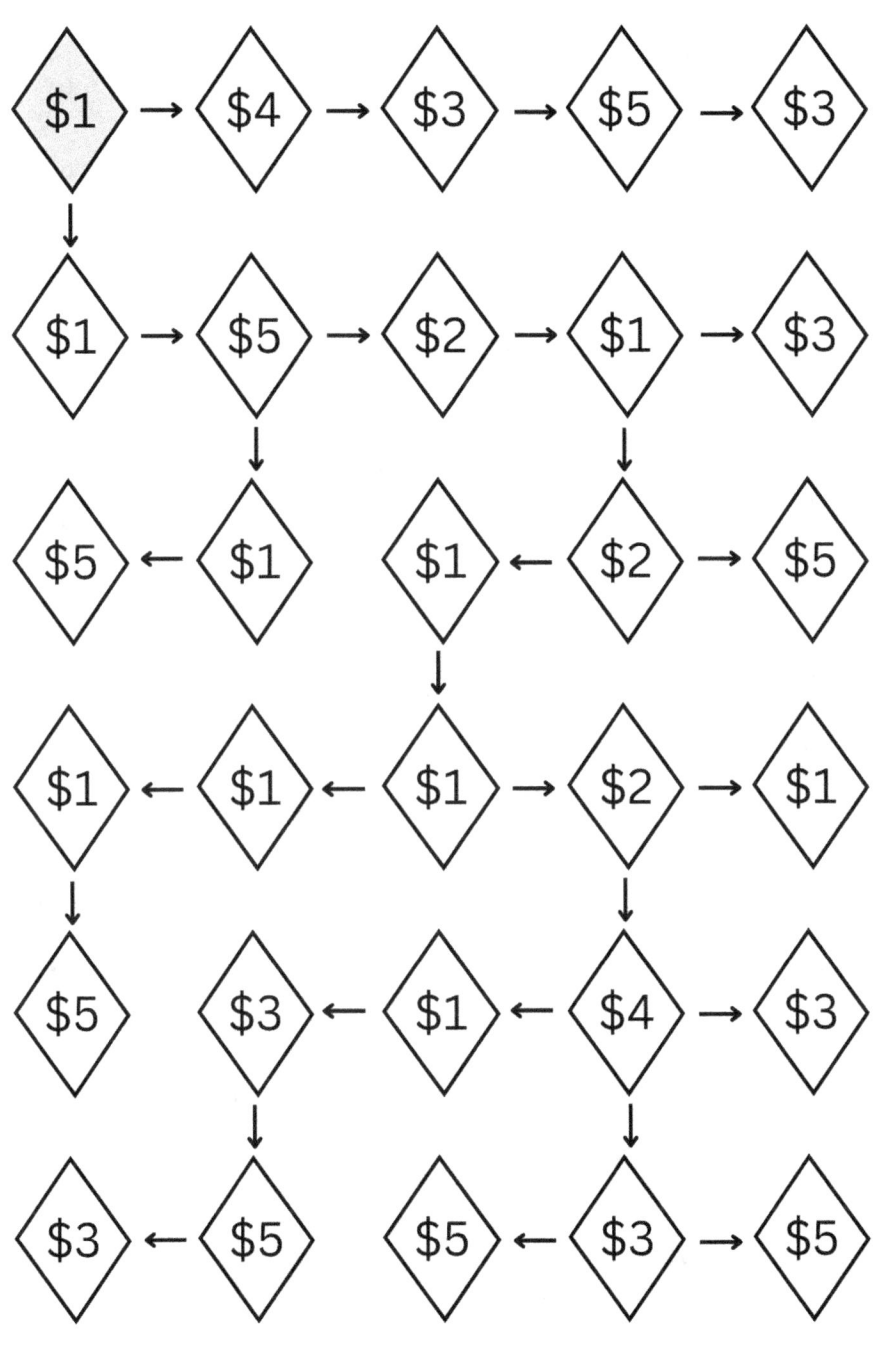

Notes: _____

Let's Save .... $100 in 48 Days

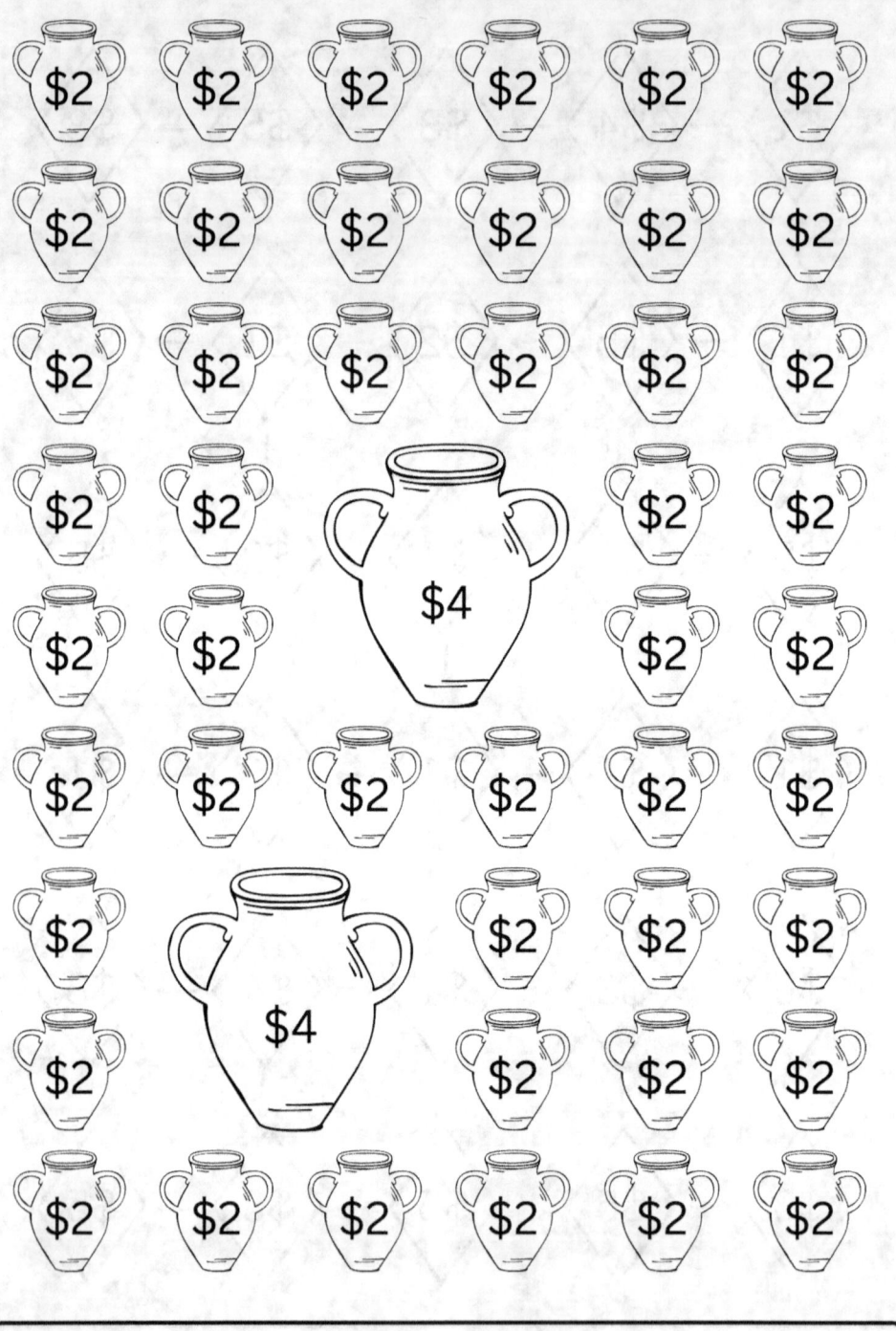

Notes: _____

Let's Save .... $60 in 17 Days

Start Small: Begin with small savings goals to build confidence and momentum.

Notes: _____
_____

Let's Save .... $85 in 35 Days

$1	$3	$2	$4	$4
$3	$3	$3	$4	$4
$4	$1	$2	$2	$3
$1	$5	$3	$4	$1
$1	$4	$5	$1	$2
$1	$2	$1	$1	$1
$4	$2	$1	$1	$1

Notes: _____
_____

Let's Save .... $65 in 21 Days

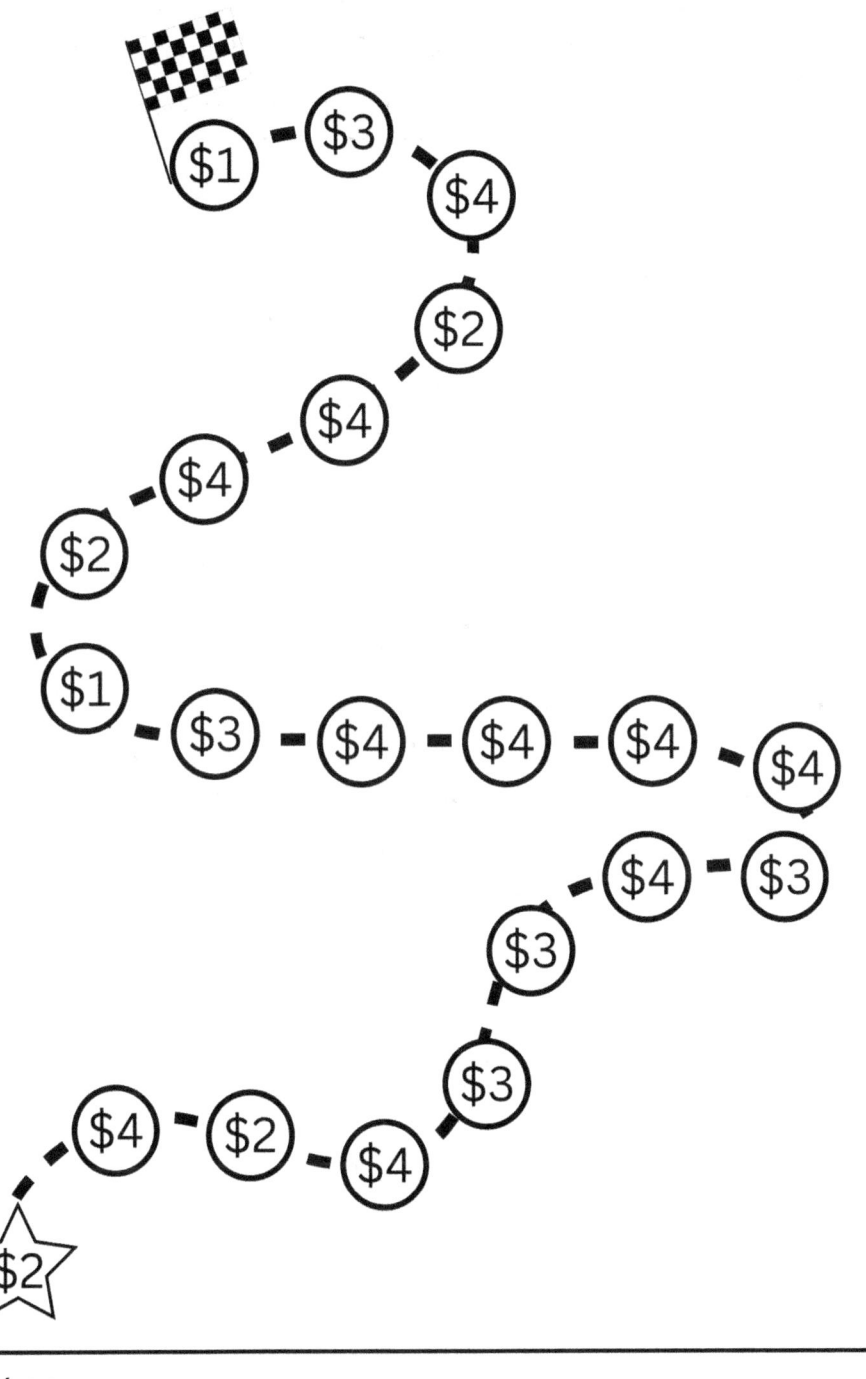

Notes: _____

Let's Save .... $75 in 21 Days

Make a Budget: Create a budget to track your income and expenses.

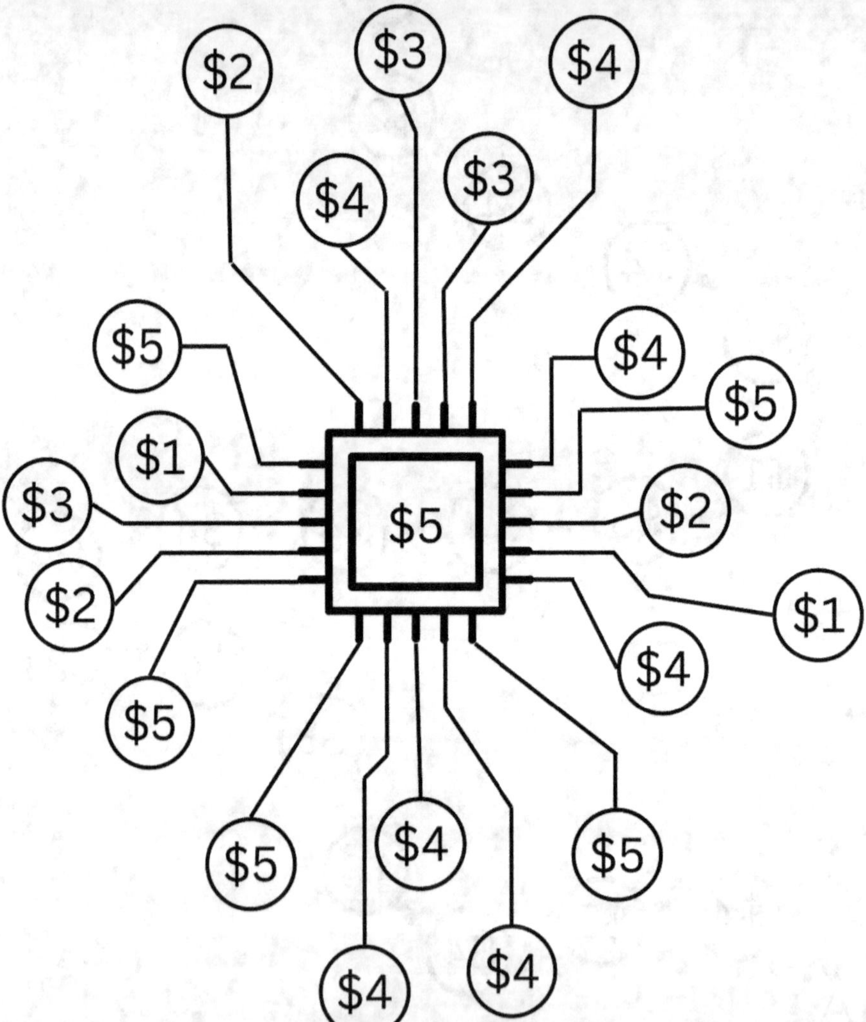

- $2, $3, $4
- $4, $3
- $5, $4, $5
- $1, $2
- $3
- $2, $1
- $5, $4
- $5
- $5, $4, $5
- $4, $4

Center: $5

Notes: _____
_____

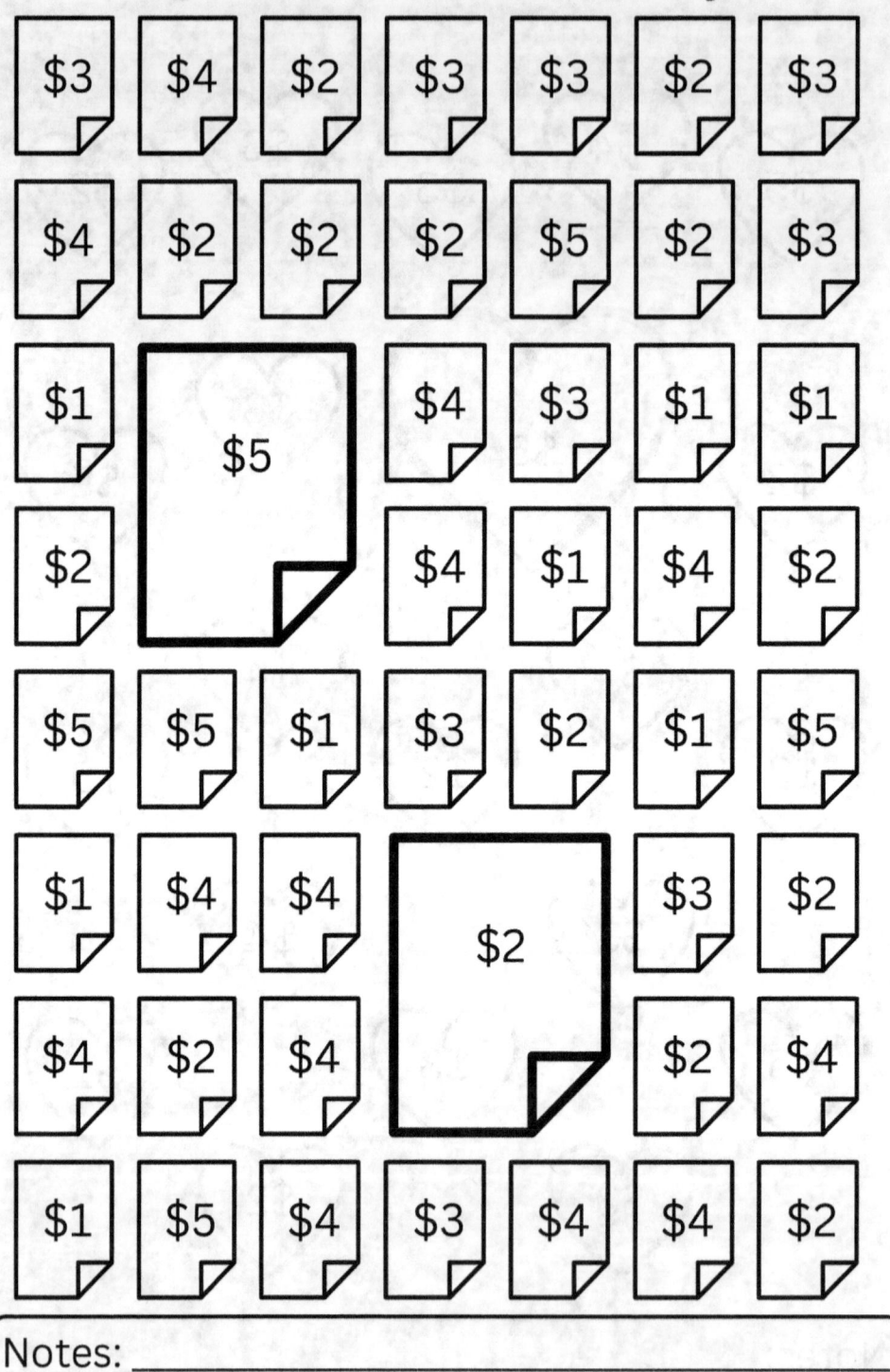

Let's Save .... $140 in 40 Days

	$5	$4	$5	$5	
$5	$3	$4	$4	$5	
	$3	$2	$3	$4	
$2	$1	$4	$1	$2	
	$5	$3	$5	$5	
$3	$1	$3	$5	$5	
	$3	$1	$5	$5	
$5	$3	$1	$2	$5	
	$1	$4	$4	$4	

Notes: _____
_____

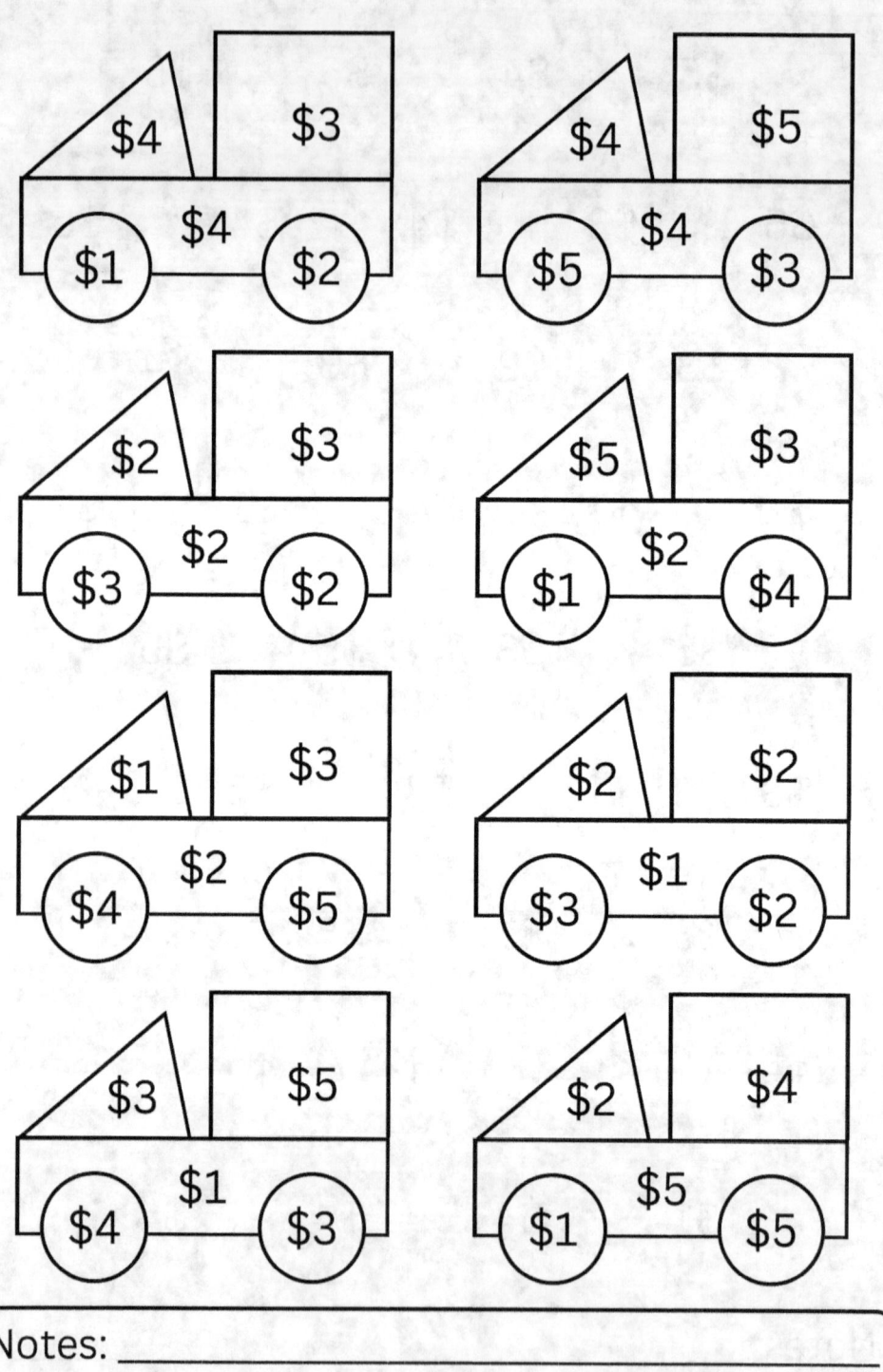

Let's Save .... $70 in 21 Days

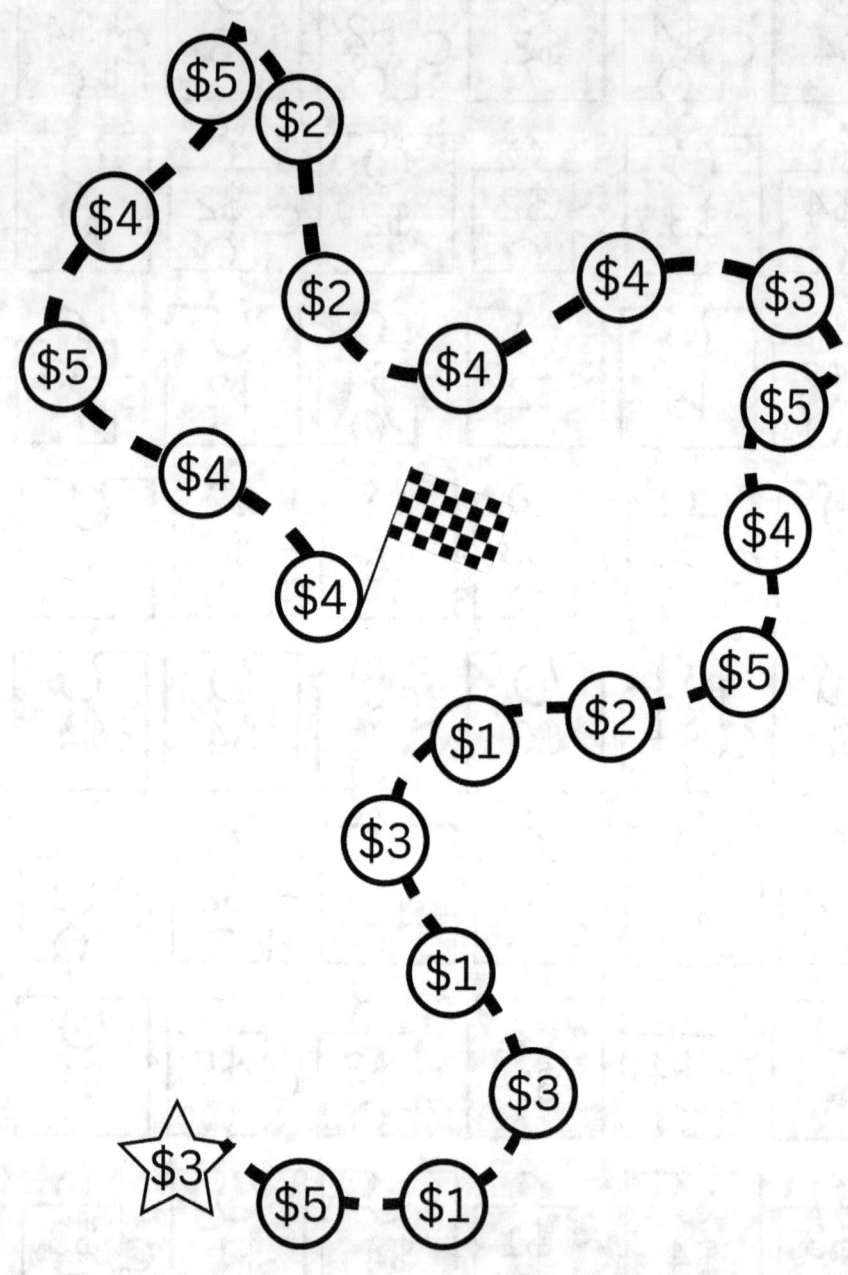

Notes: _____
_____

Let's Save .... $115 in 40 Days

Notes: _____
_____

Let's Save .... $80 in 35 Days

$2	$4	$3	$1	$3
$3	$3	$1	$3	$3
$3	$2	$3	$2	$1

Prioritize Needs Over Wants: Distinguish between essential and non-essential expenses.

$3	$1	$2	$1	$2
$3	$3	$3	$3	$3
$3	$1	$3	$1	$3
$1	$3	$1	$1	$2

Notes: _____
_____

Let's Save .... $185 in 62 Days

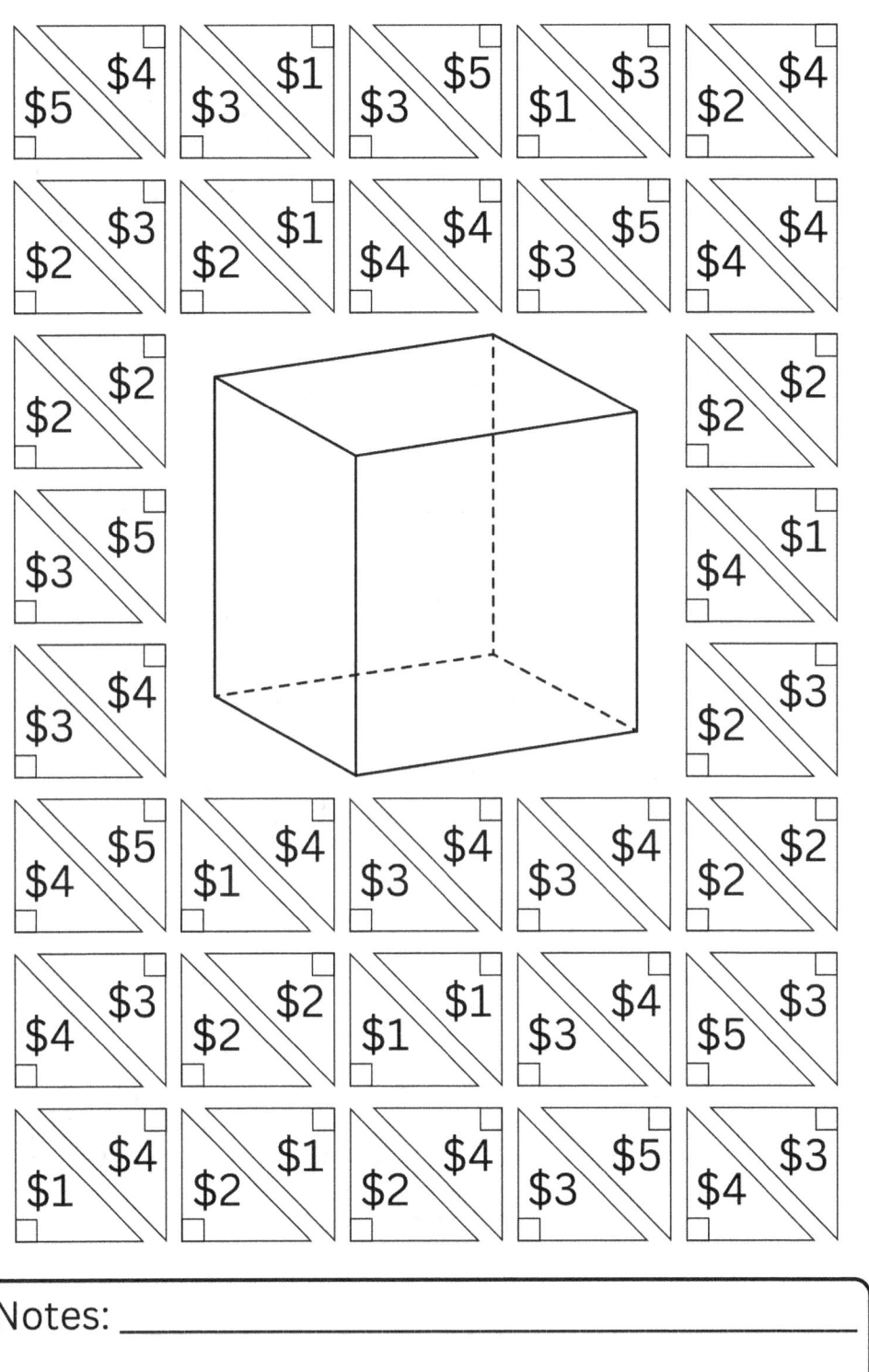

Notes: _____
_____

Let's Save .... $55 in 25 Days

$2	$4	$2	$3	$5
$4		$1		$3
$1	$3	$2	$1	$3

> **Be Patient**: Saving takes time and patience, so stay committed to your goals.

$1	$2	$1	$2	$1
	$1		$1	
$3	$3	$3	$1	$2

Notes: _____
_____

Let's Save .... $155 in 45 Days

Notes: _____

Let's Save .... $50 in 20 Days

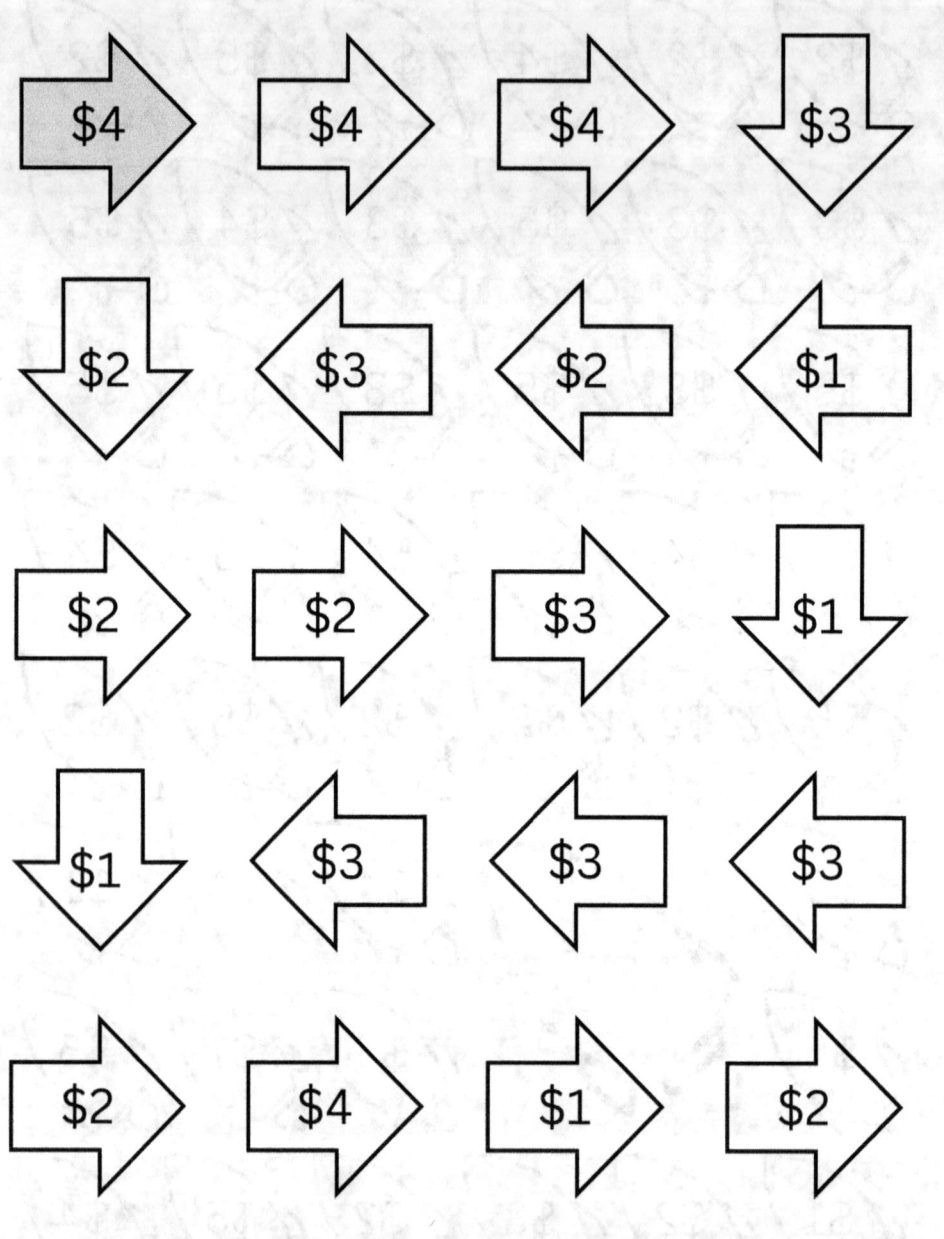

Notes: _____
_____

Let's Save .... $95 in 42 Days

Notes: _____
_____

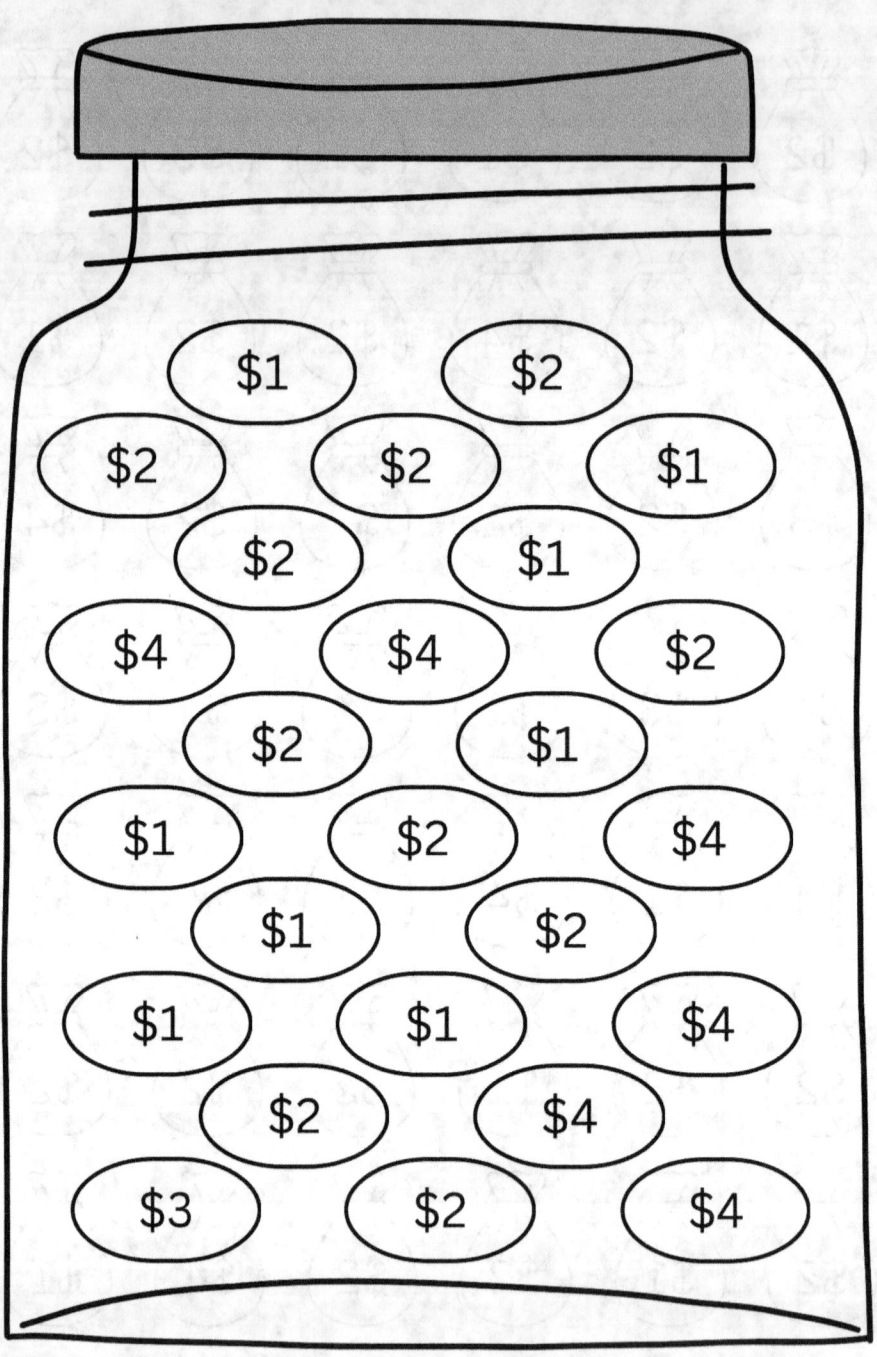

Let's Save .... $100 in 33 Days

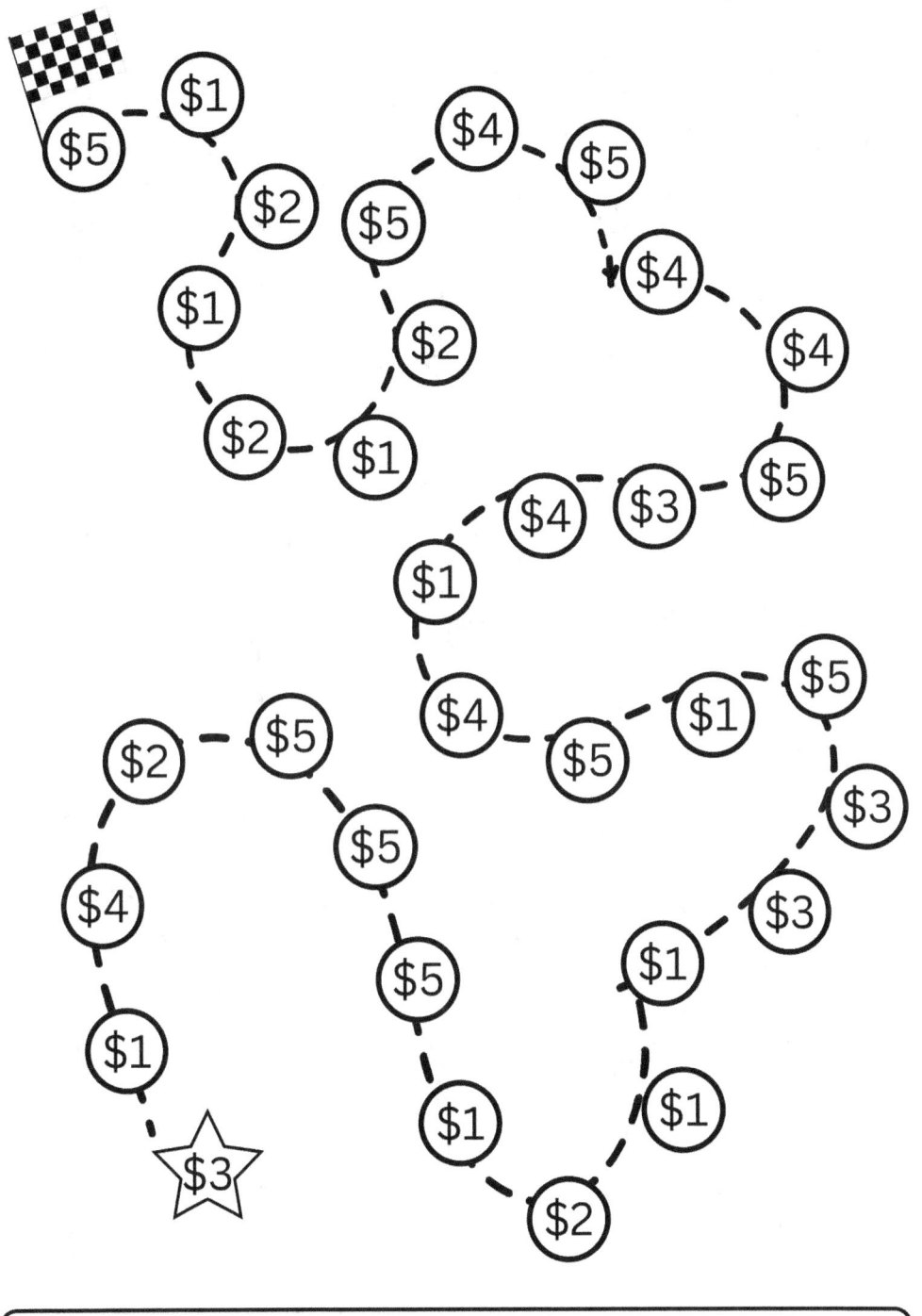

Notes: _____

Let's Save .... $35 in 15 Days

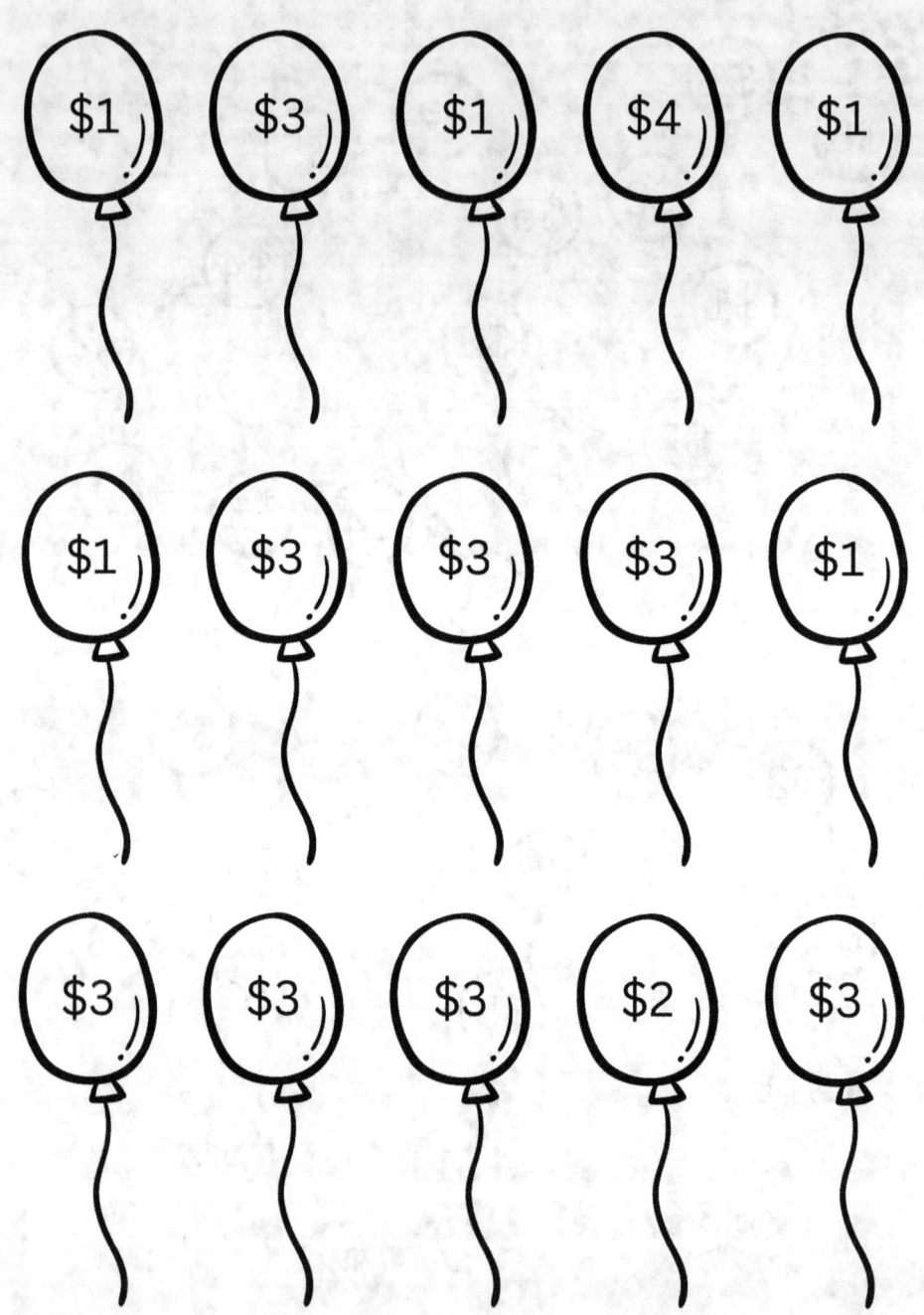

Notes: _____
_____

Let's Save .... $95 in 39 Days

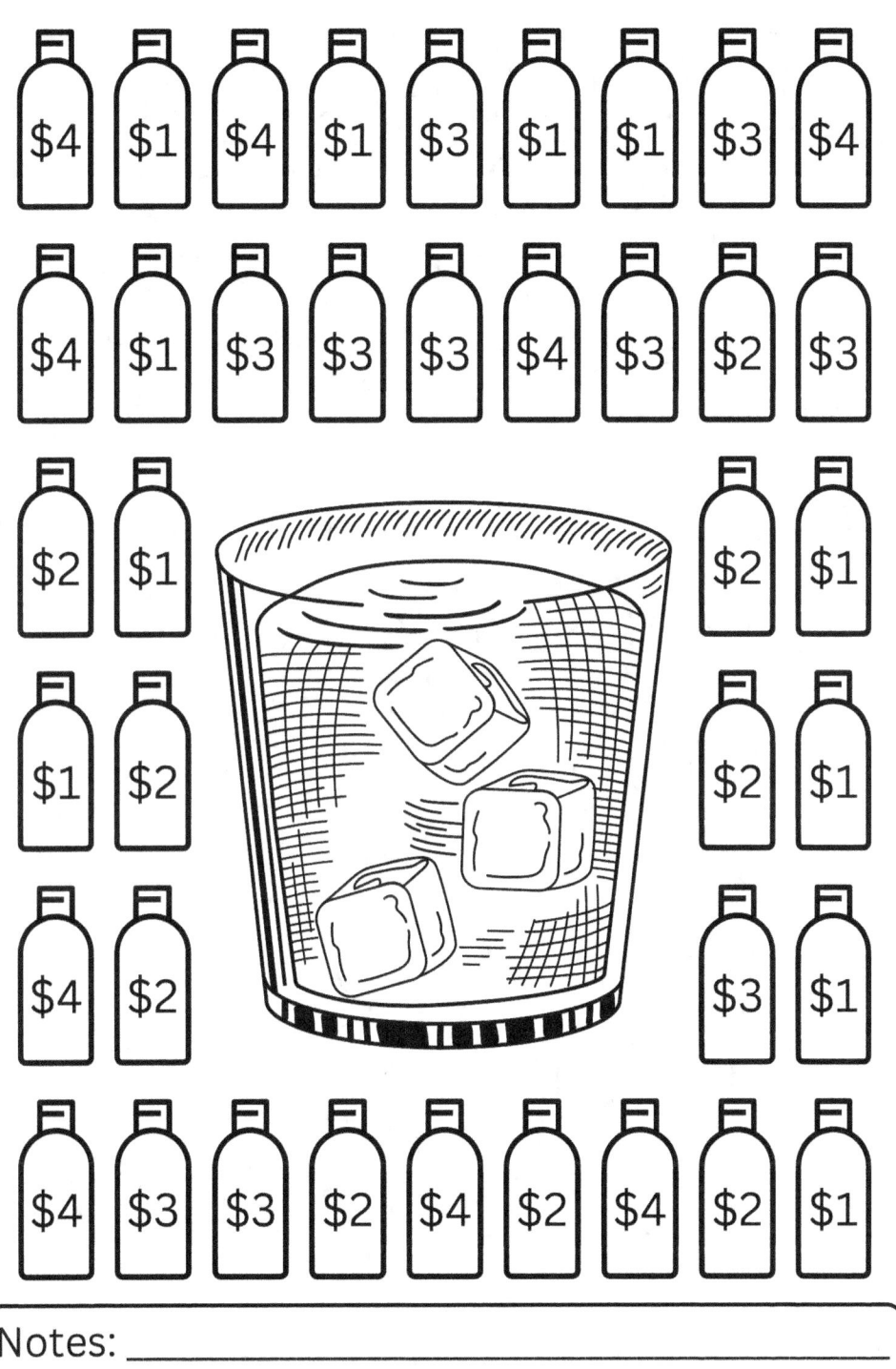

Notes: _____
_____

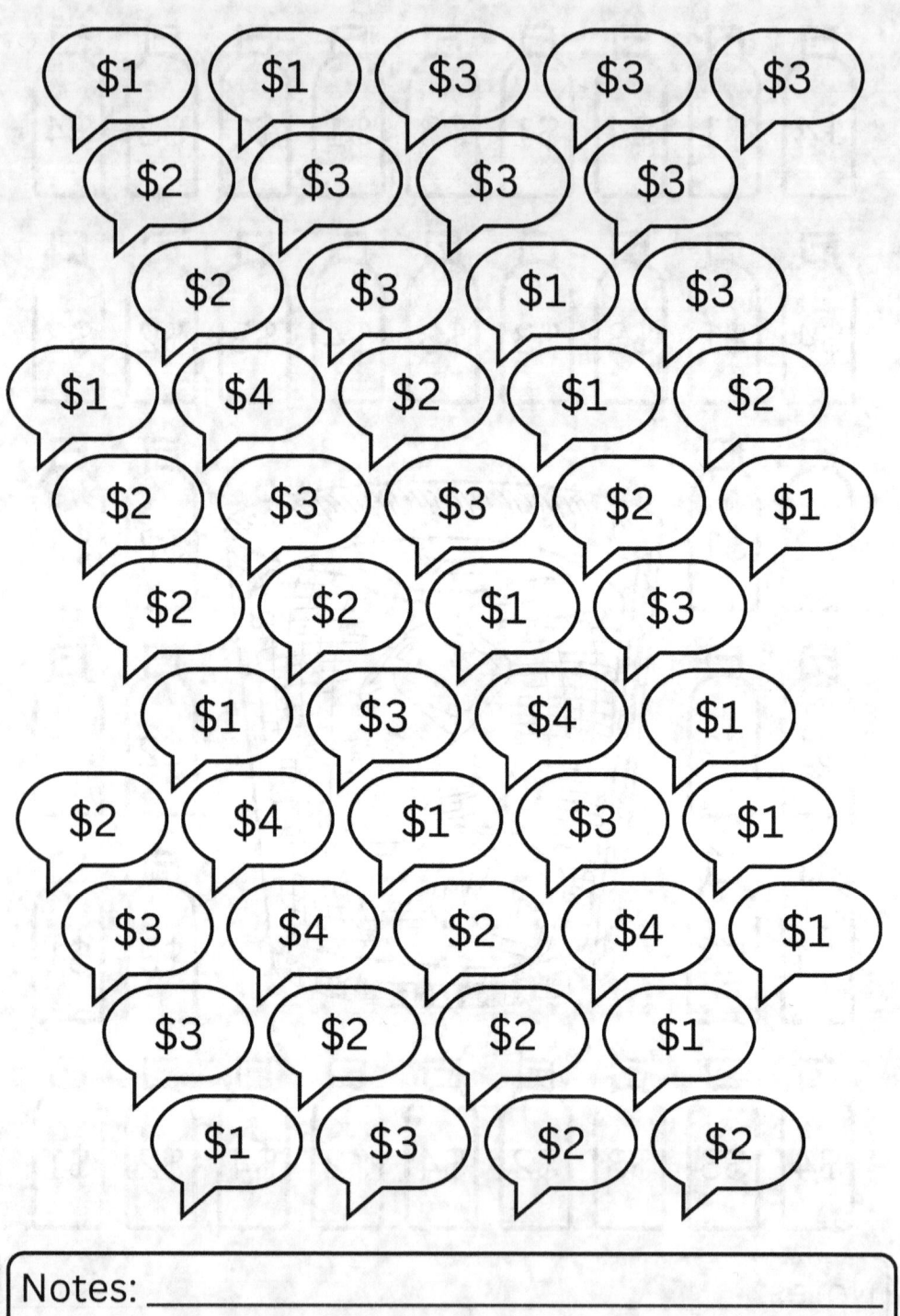

Let's Save .... $90 in 27 Days

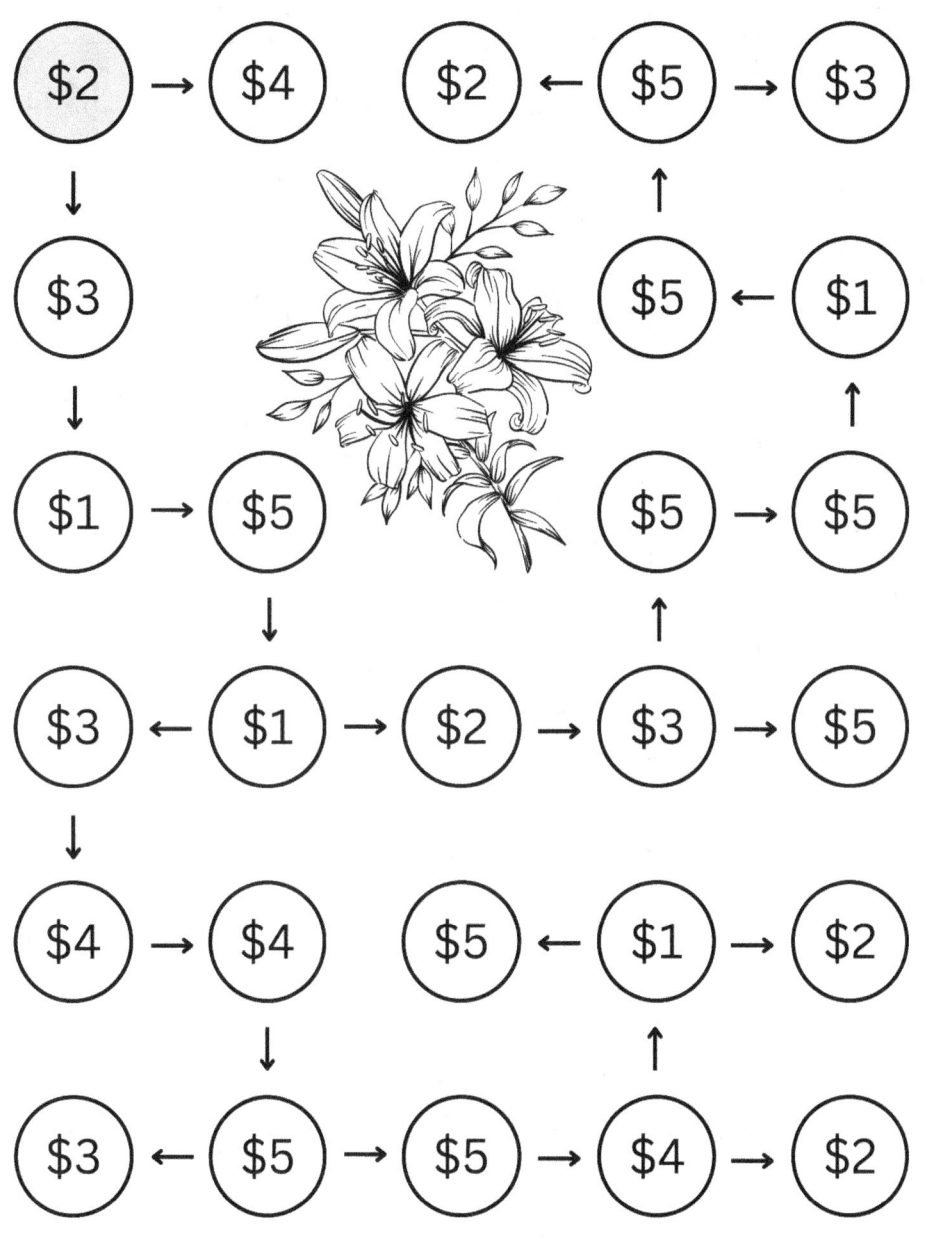

Notes: _____
_____

Let's Save .... $85 in 36 Days

Notes: _____
_____

Let's Save .... $170 in 63 Days

Notes: _____
_____

Let's Save …. $80 in 35 Days

Notes: _____
_____

Let's Save .... $320 in 118 Days

Notes: _____

Let's Save .... $85 in 32 Days

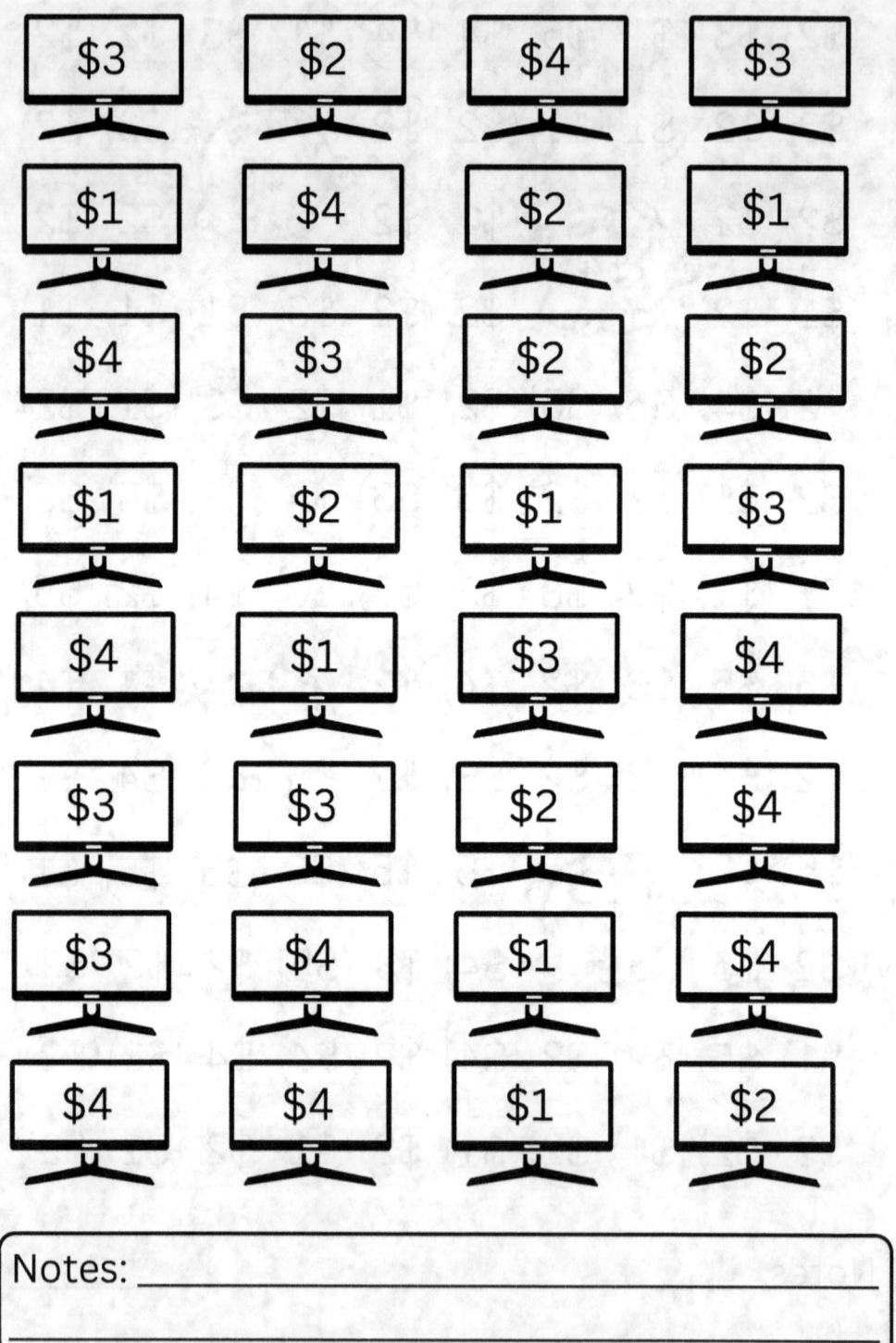

Notes: _____

Let's Save .... $145 in 41 Days

Notes: _____

Let's Save .... $140 in 42 Days

Notes: _____
_____

Let's Save .... $115 in 40 Days

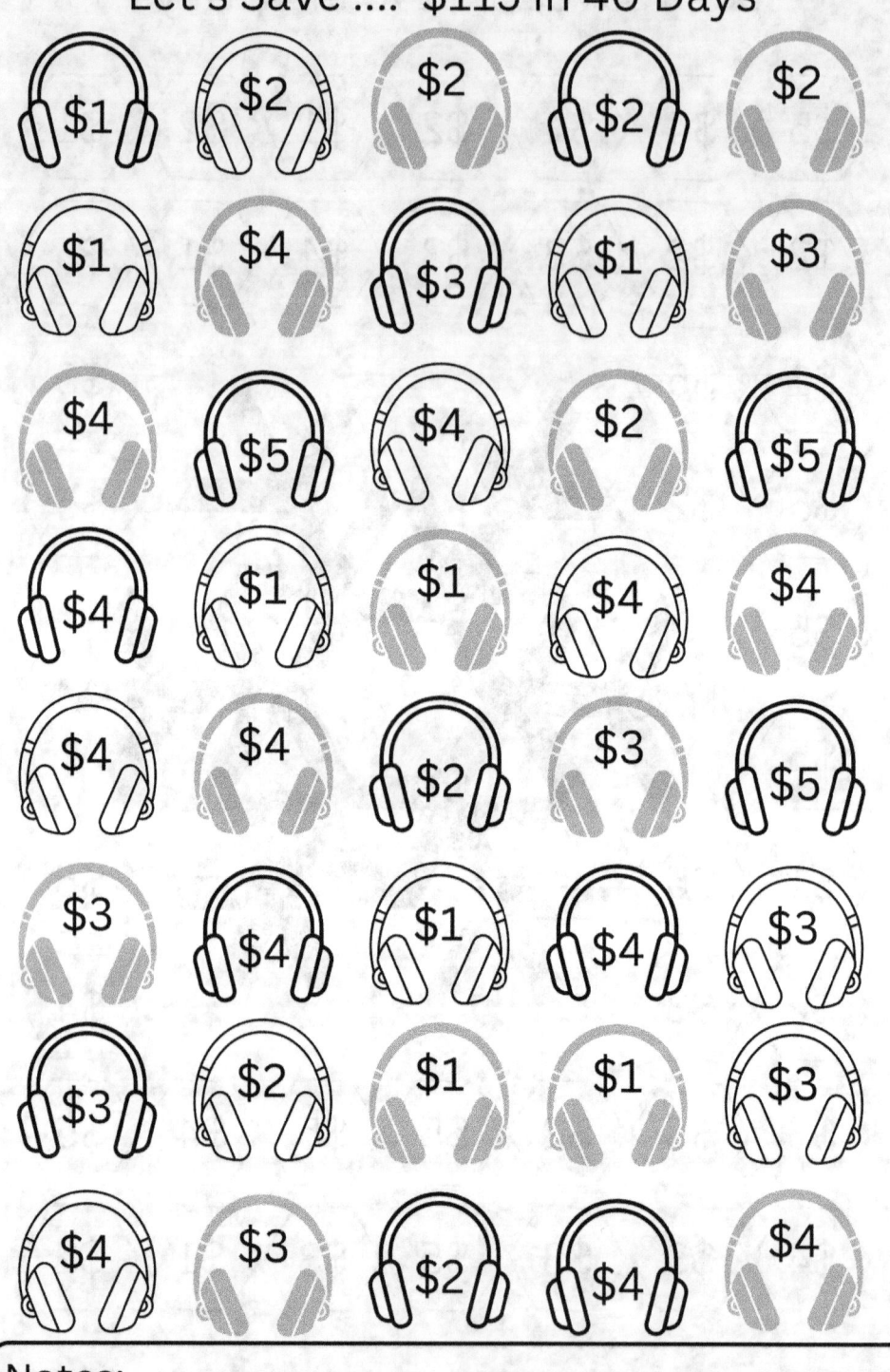

Notes: _____
_____

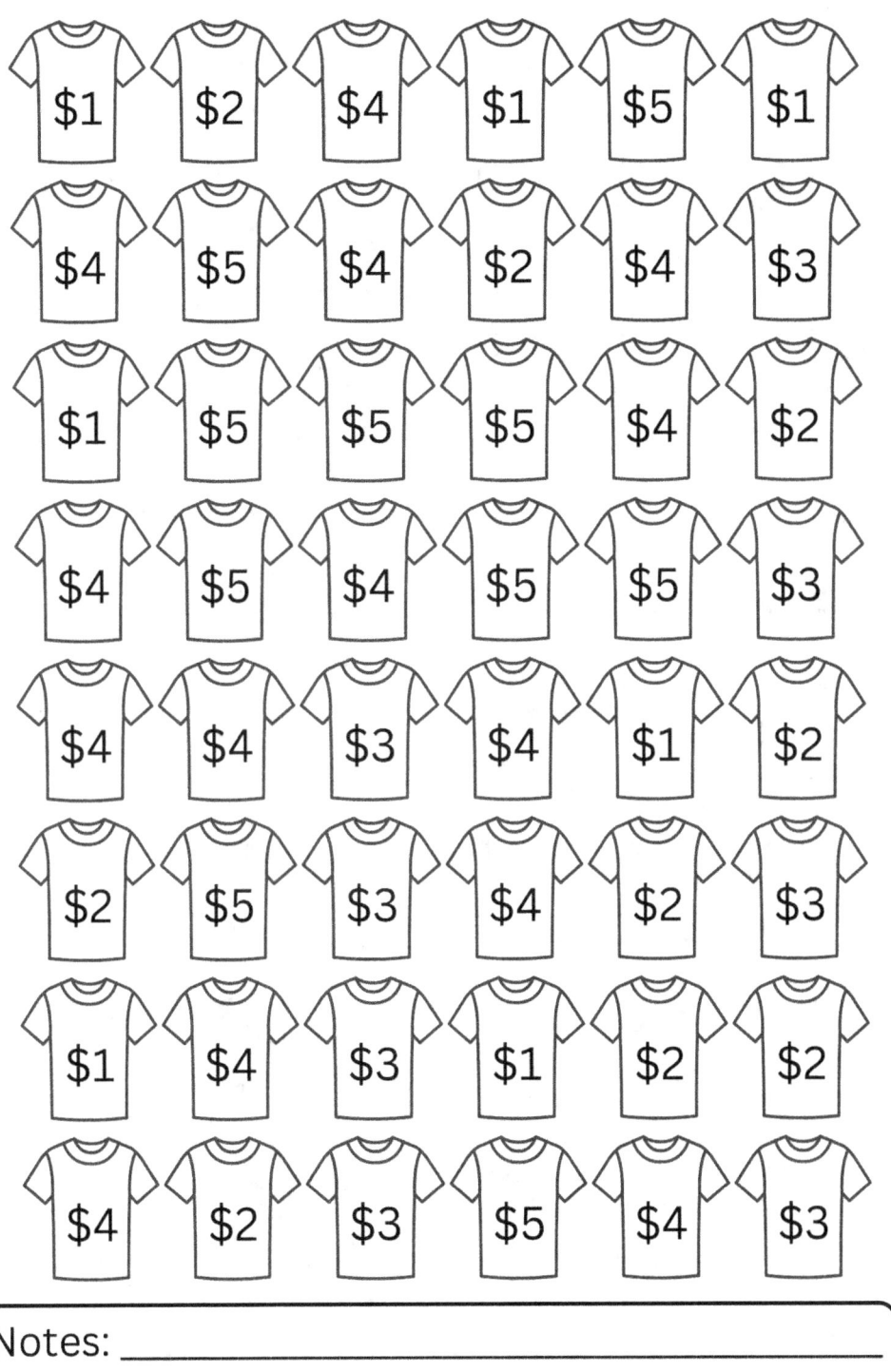

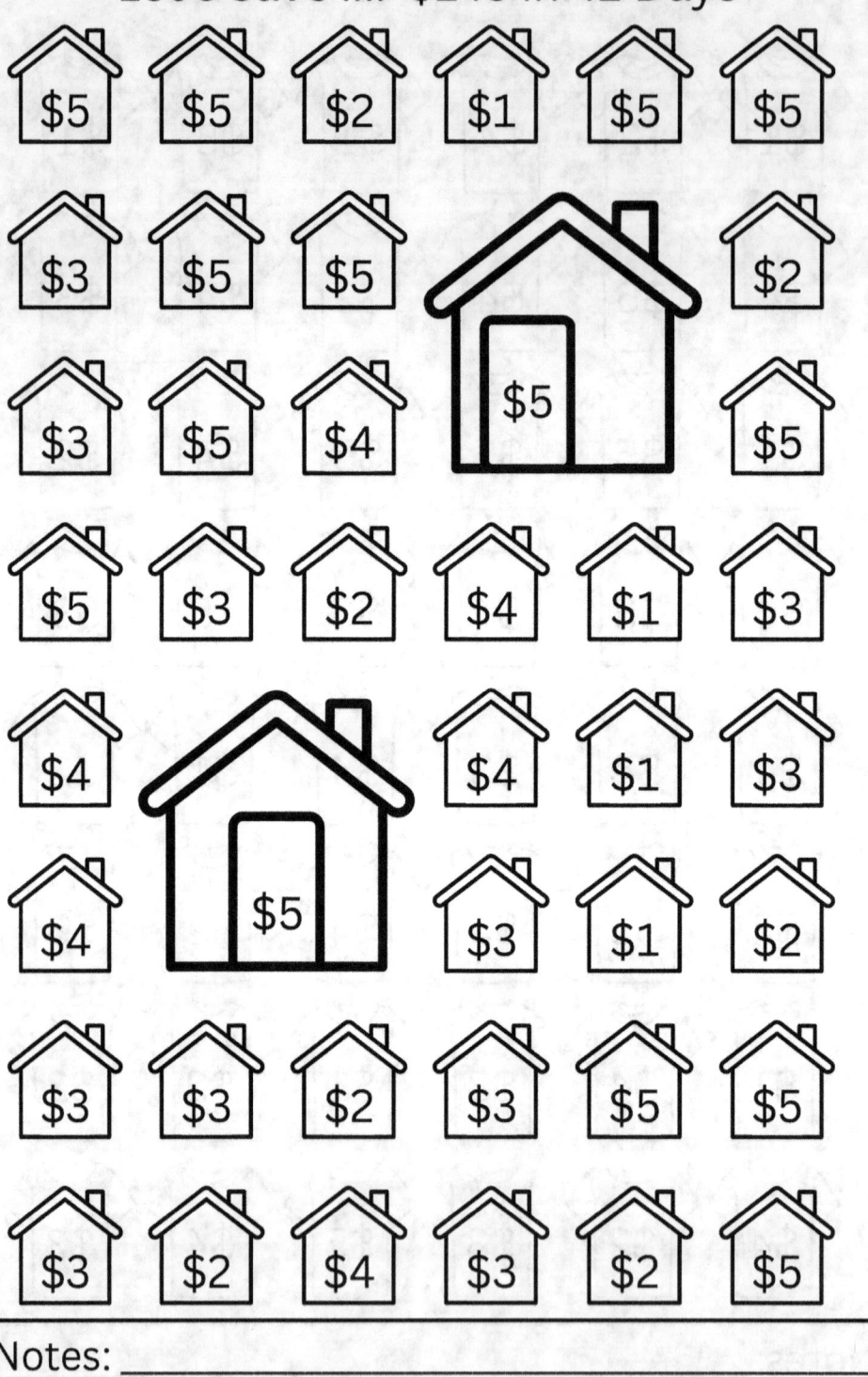

Let's Save .... $185 in 60 Days

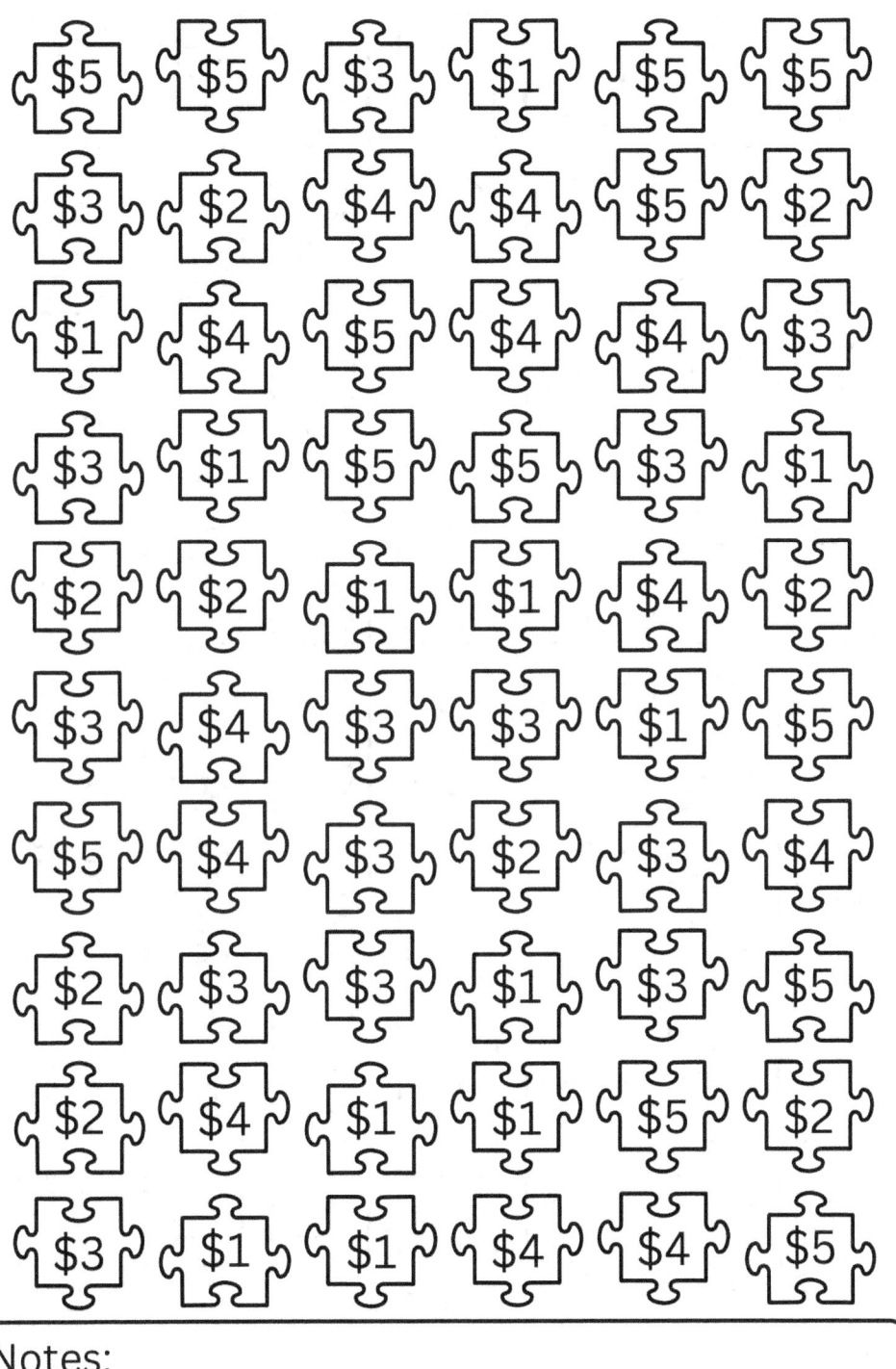

Notes: _____
_____

Let's Save .... $185 in 56 Days

Notes: _____
_____

Let's Save .... $260 in 85 Days

$1 $2 $4 $2 $3 $5 $2
 $2 $1 $5 $5 $1 $1
$5 $3 $3 $5 $5 $2 $4
 $4 $1 $2 $2 $3 $1
$5 $4 $3 $4 $5 $5 $5
 $1 $2 $1 $2 $4 $4
$5 $4 $3 $5 $4 $2 $1
 $2 $1 $1 $5 $1 $3
$3 $4 $5 $2 $3 $3 $2
 $3 $3 $2 $3 $4 $5
$5 $5 $5 $3 $4 $2 $2
 $3 $3 $1 $1 $3 $3
$5 $3 $2 $4 $4 $3 $1

Notes: _____
_____

Let's Save .... $235 in 79 Days

$2	$4	$4	$1	$2	$3	$4
$1	$1	$1	$1	$4	$4	$5
$1	$4	$3	$2	$4	$4	$3
$1	$3	$2	$2	$2	$5	$2
$2	$2				$1	$5
$2	$5				$5	$2
$5	$1				$2	$4
$5	$2				$2	$4
$4	$2	$3	$5	$4	$4	$1
$3	$3	$3	$4	$2	$3	4
$5	$4	$3	$2	$2	$4	$5
$1	$5	$5	$4	$3	$2	$4
$2	$3	$4	$1	$2	$2	$3

Notes: _____
_____

Let's Save .... $125 in 34 Days

$5 $5 $2 $3 $4
$4 $4 $5 $4
$3 $5 $5
$5 $4 $1 $2 $2
$4 $5 $4 $2 $5
$5 $4 $5
$1 $5 $1 $5
$3 $3 $2 $5 $3

Notes: _____
_____

Let's Save .... $220 in 64 Days

$5	$3	$3	$4	$1	$5	$4	$2
$2	$1	$4	$4	$5	$4	$5	$1
$1	$4	$2	$5	$5	$4	$3	$5
$4	$4	$2	$5	$5	$5	$5	$3
$2	$3	$1	$5	$5	$5	$1	$1
$5	$2	$4	$1	$5	$2	$5	$1
$5	$2	$5	$5	$4	$2	$5	$5
$1	$1	$2	$4	$5	$4	$5	$2

Notes: _____
_____

Let's Save .... $200 in 77 Days

Notes: _____

Let's Save .... $170 in 56 Days

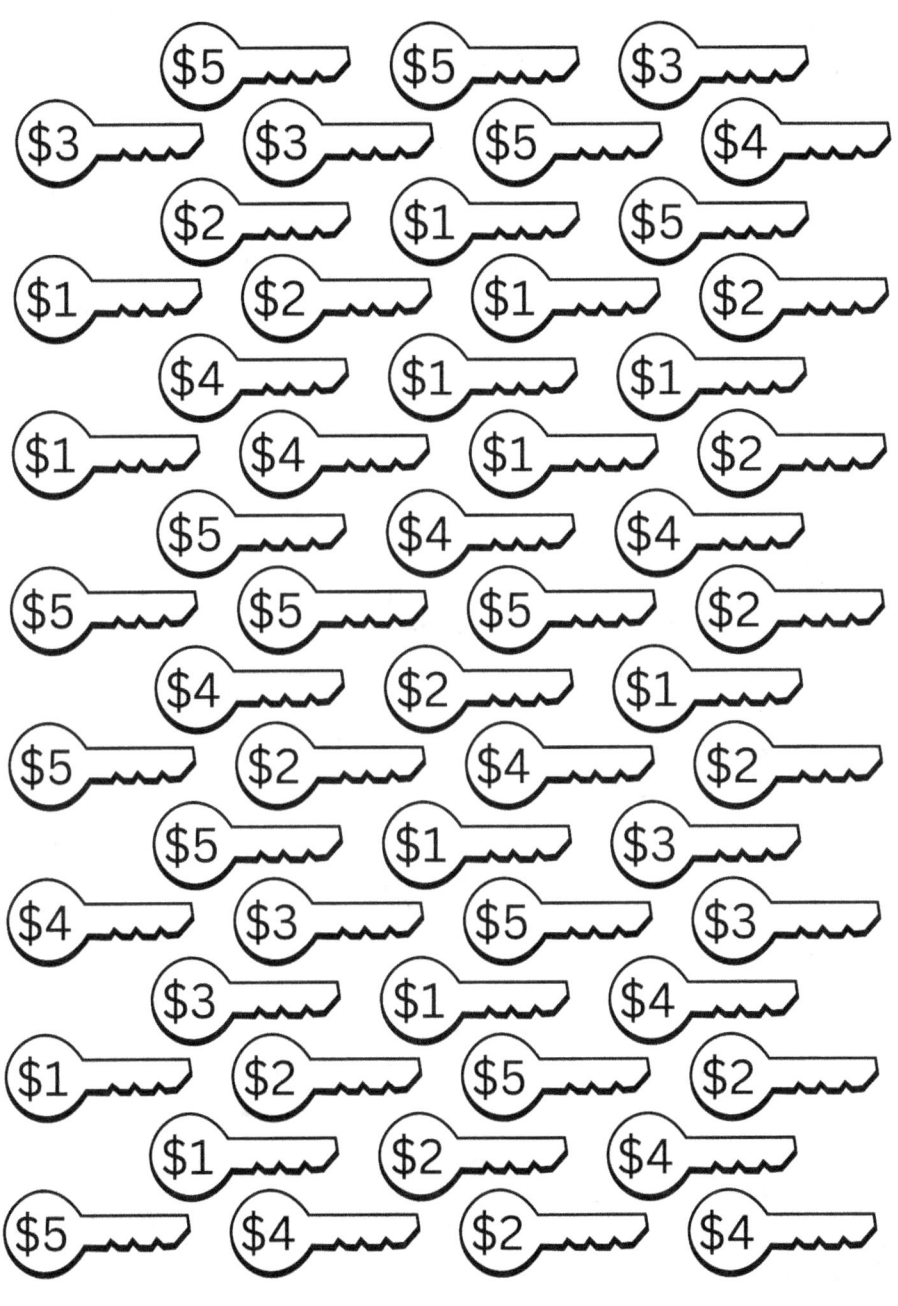

Notes: _____
_____

Let's Save .... $100 in 34 Days

$5	$1	$4	$3
$1	$2	$5	$1
$1	$3	$2	$5
$4	$4	$5	$1	$1
$1	$5	$2	$2
$4	$4	$3	$2
$2	$5	$3	$5	$4
$2	$4	$3	$1

Notes: _____

Let's Save .... $60 in 18 Days

Let's Save .... $60 in 20 Days

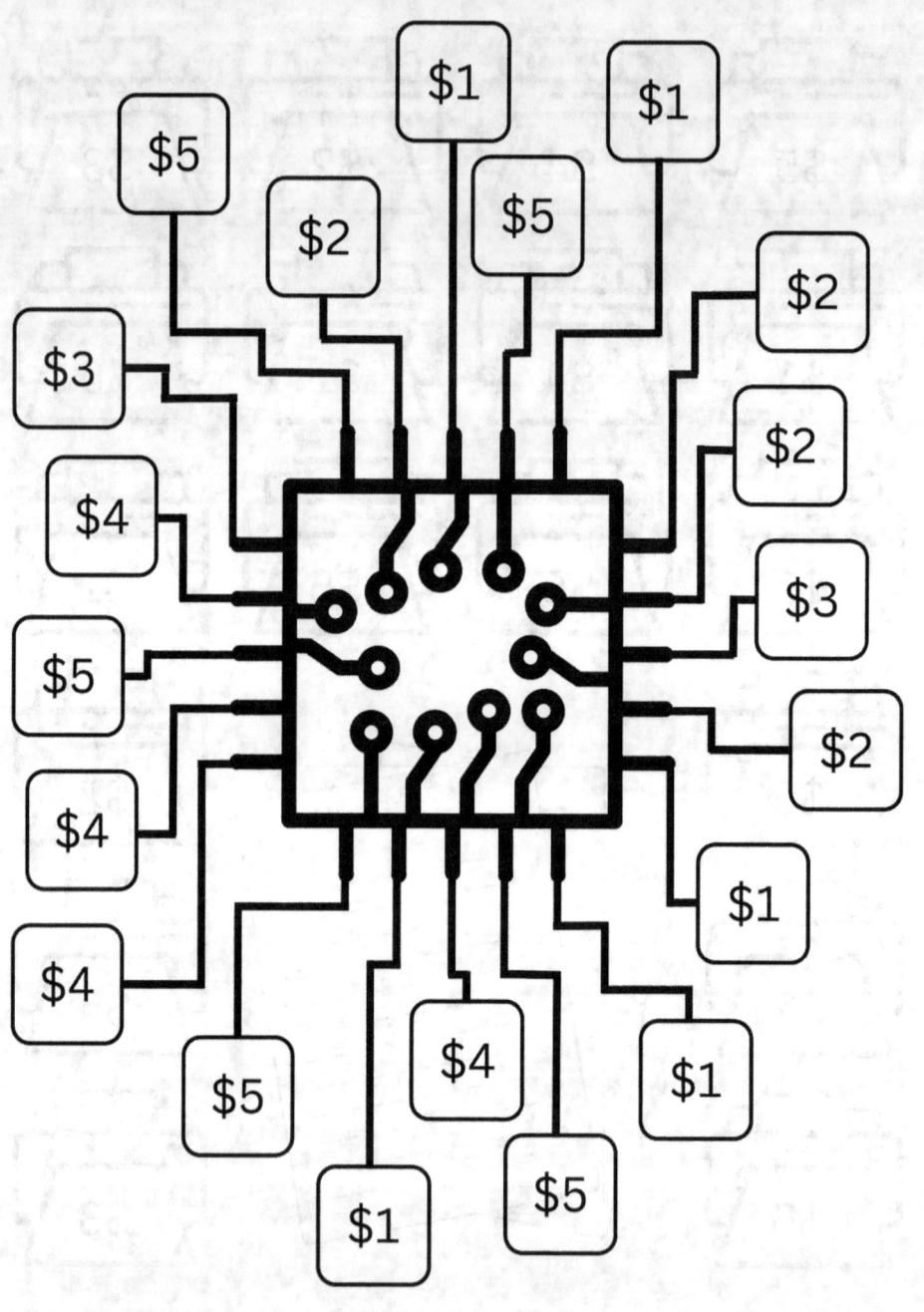

Notes: _____
_____

THE REAL LOW INCOME SAVINGS CHALLENGES
JUST $5 OR LESS PER DAY

We would greatly appreciate it if you could provide a review as we love to receive feedback from our customers. Thank you!

★ ★ ★ ★ ★

You can use this link:
https://www.amazon.com/review/create-review/?asin=B0C6BQL5V2

Get your Free download

https://www.pagetitans.com/?page=000S59

Let's Save .... $70 in 21 Days

Notes: _____

Let's Save .... $45 in 14 Days

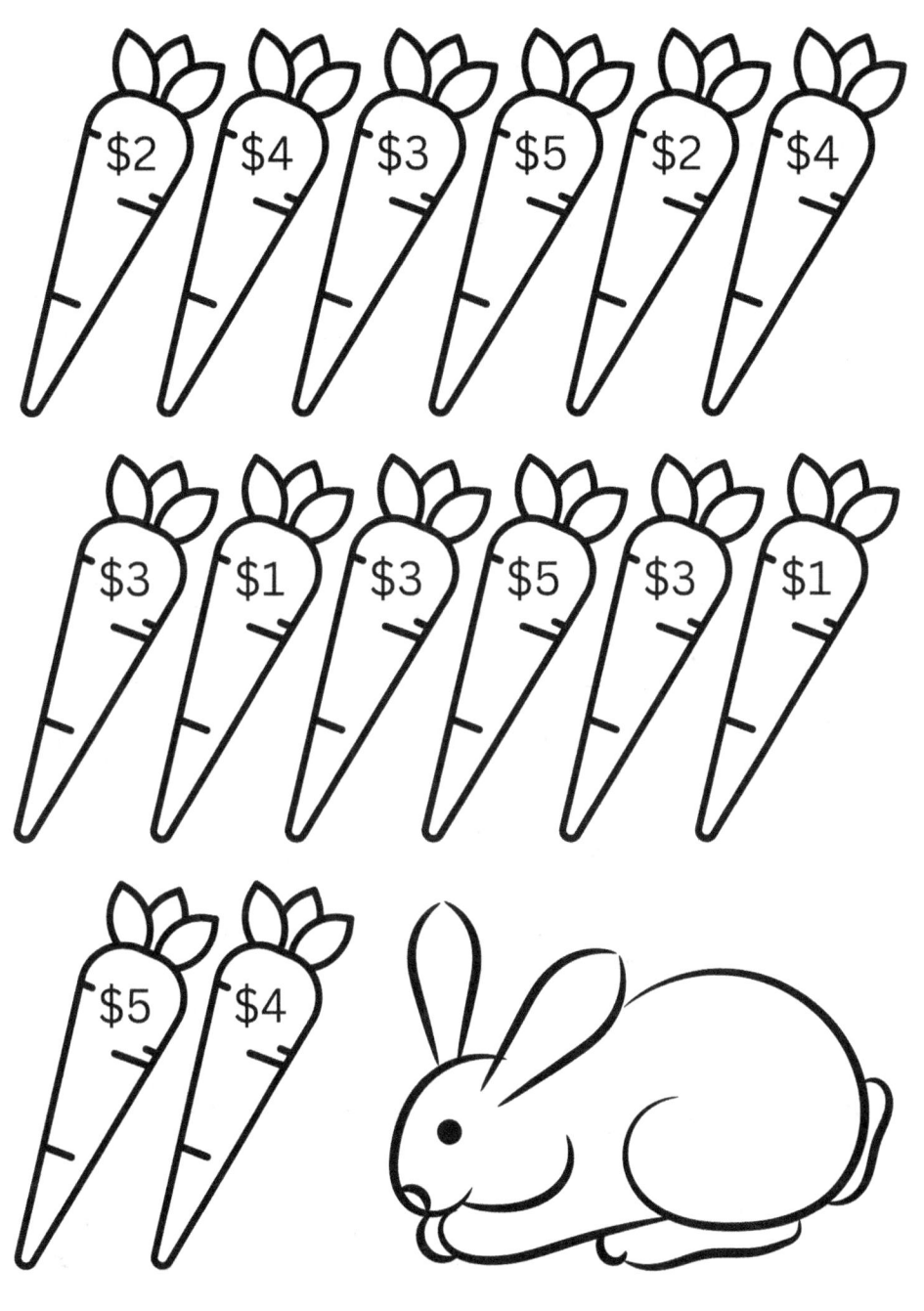

Notes: _____

Let's Save .... $210 in 64 Days

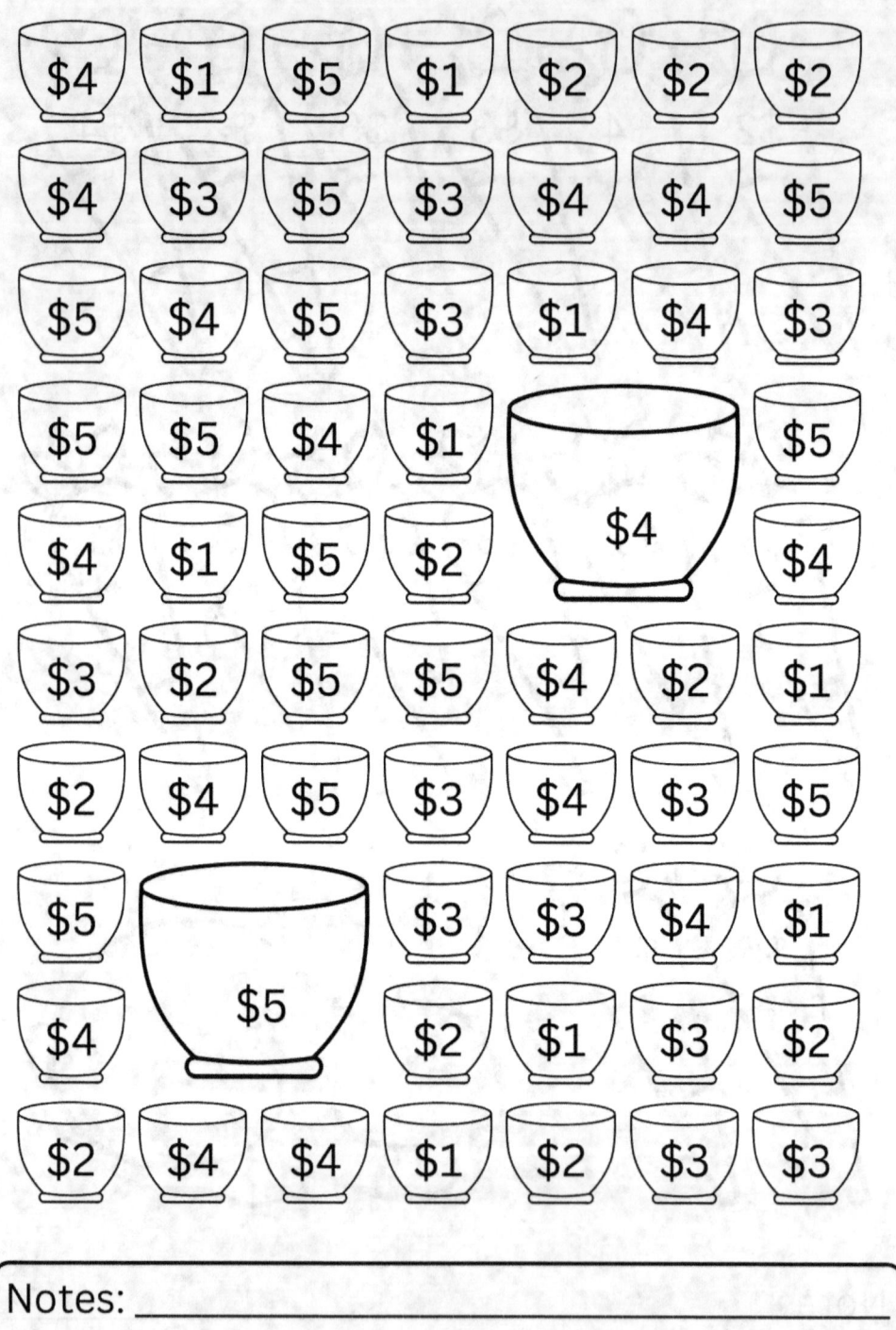

Notes: _____
_____

Let's Save .... $140 in 42 Days

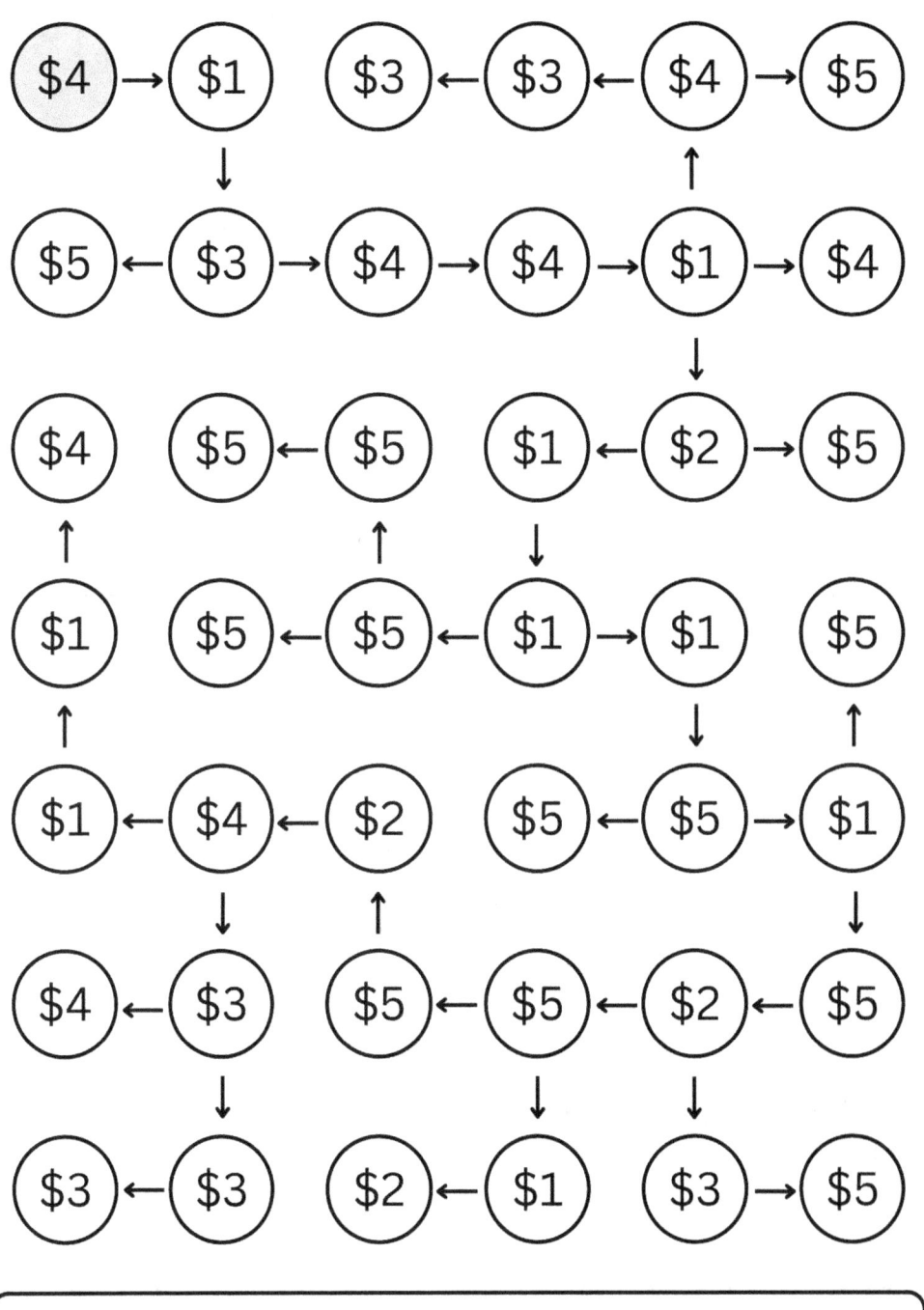

Notes: _____
_____

Let's Save .... $115 in 39 Days

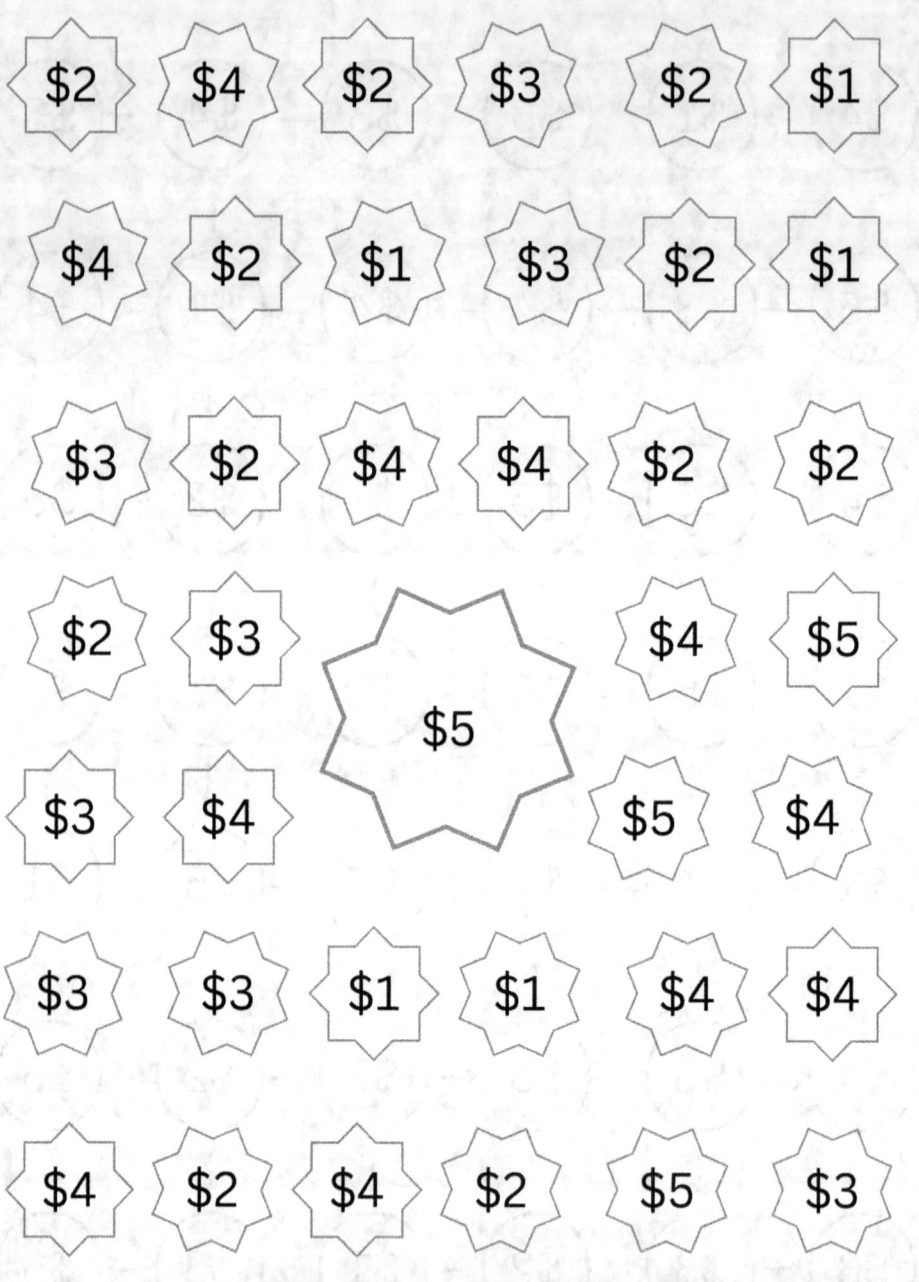

Notes: _____

Let's Save .... $120 in 42 Days

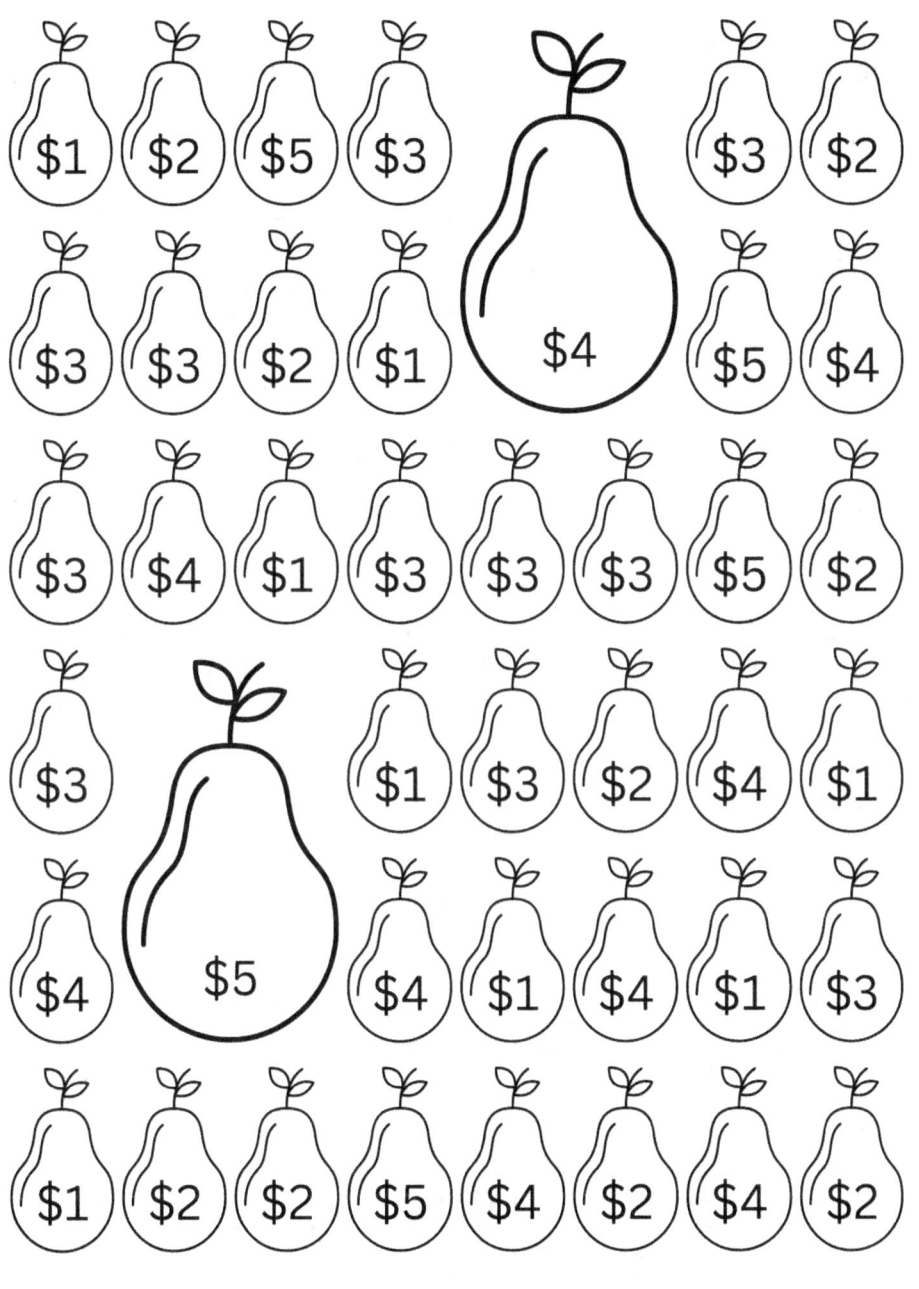

Let's Save .... $105 in 35 Days

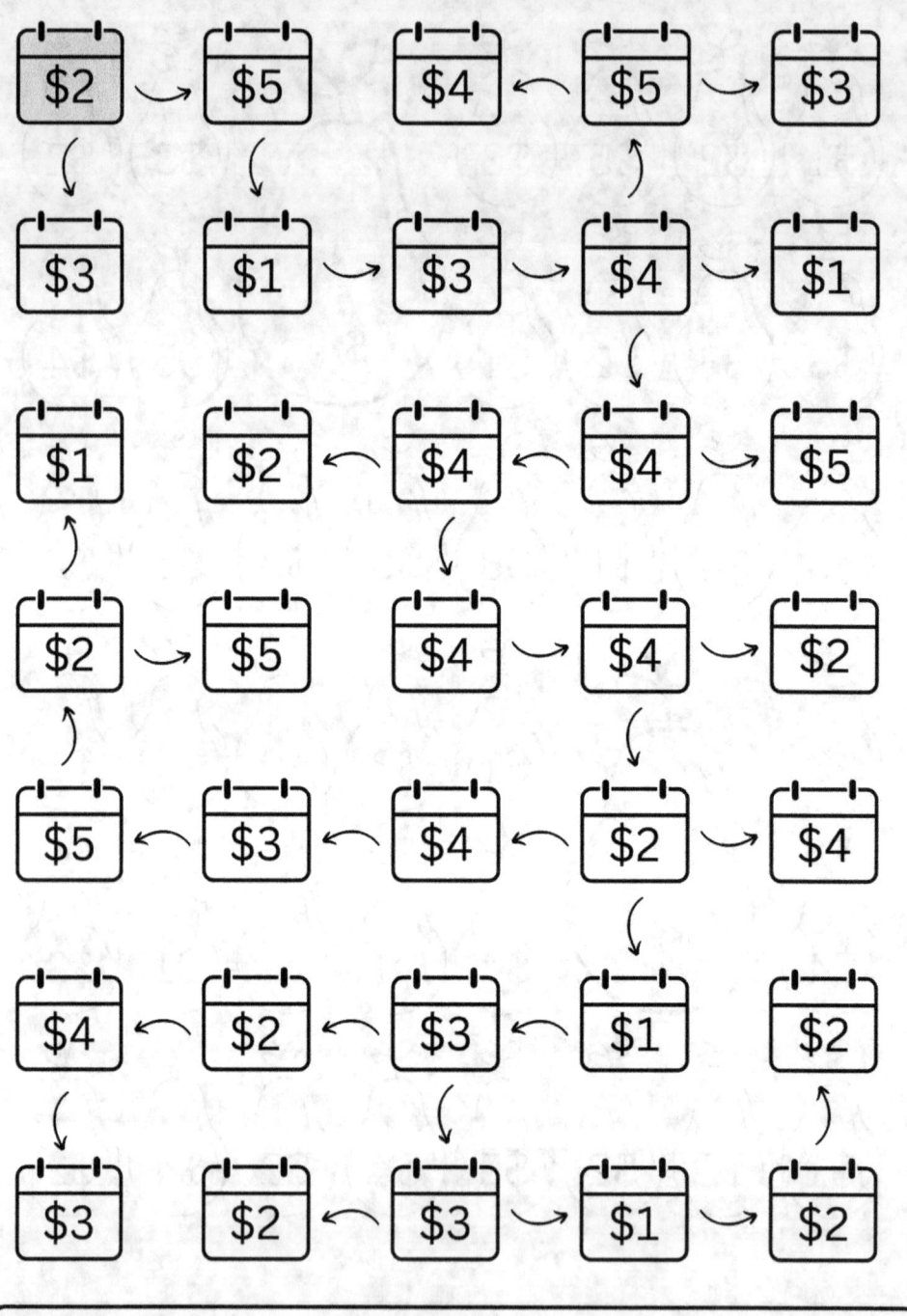

Notes: _____

Let's Save .... $245 in 93 Days

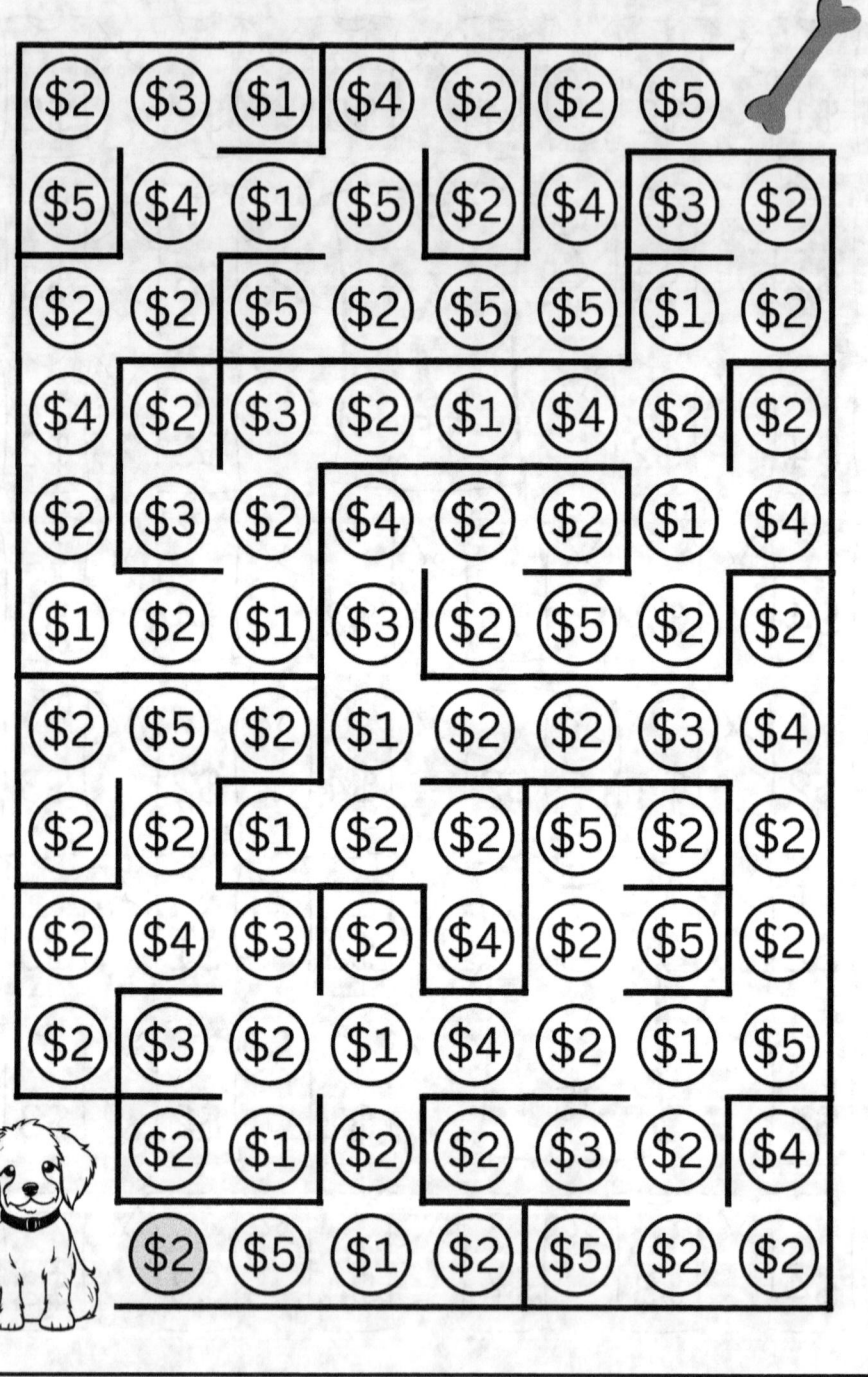

Notes: _____

Let's Save .... $85 in 27 Days

Notes: _____
_____

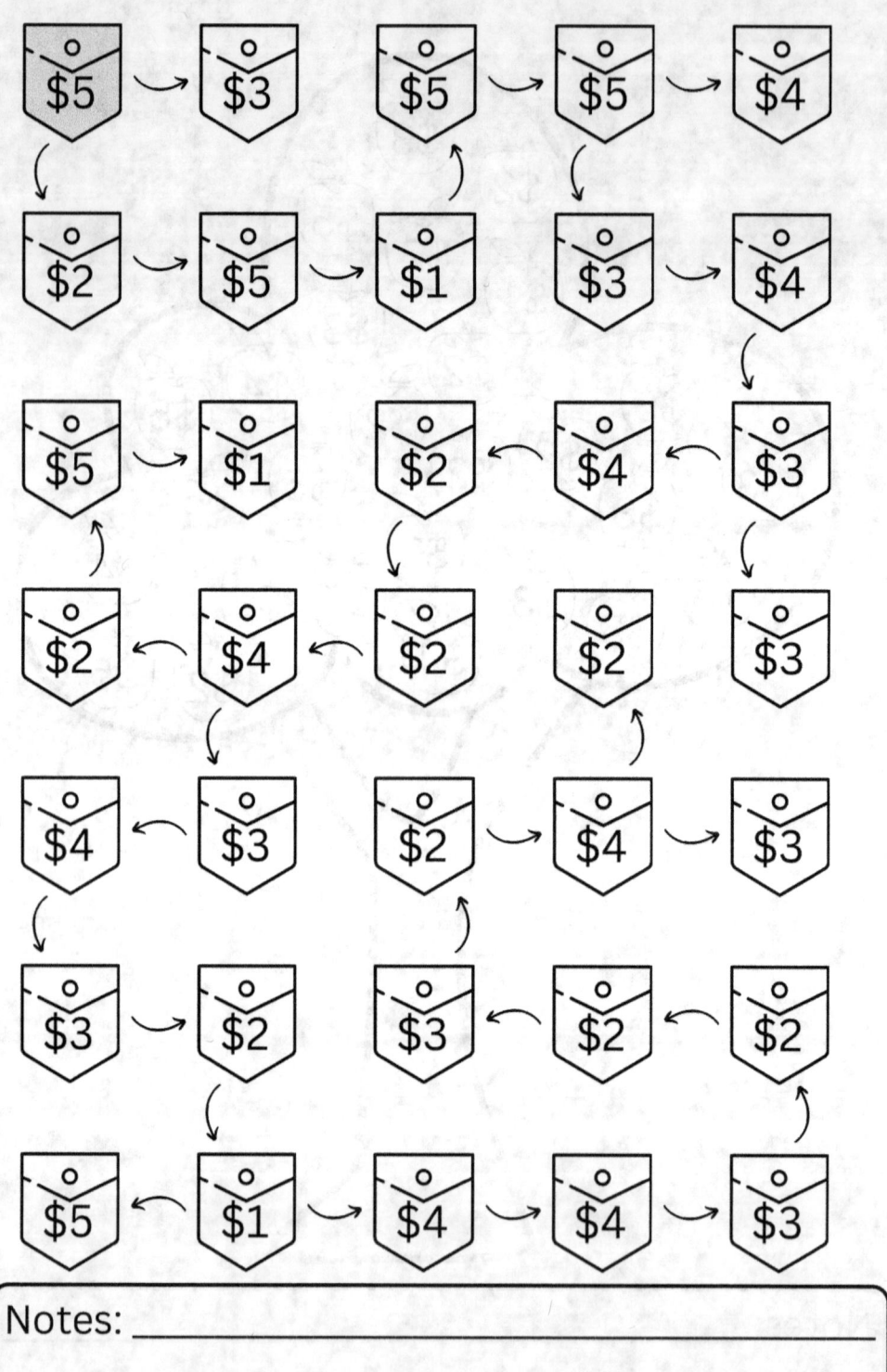

Let's Save .... $160 in 53 Days

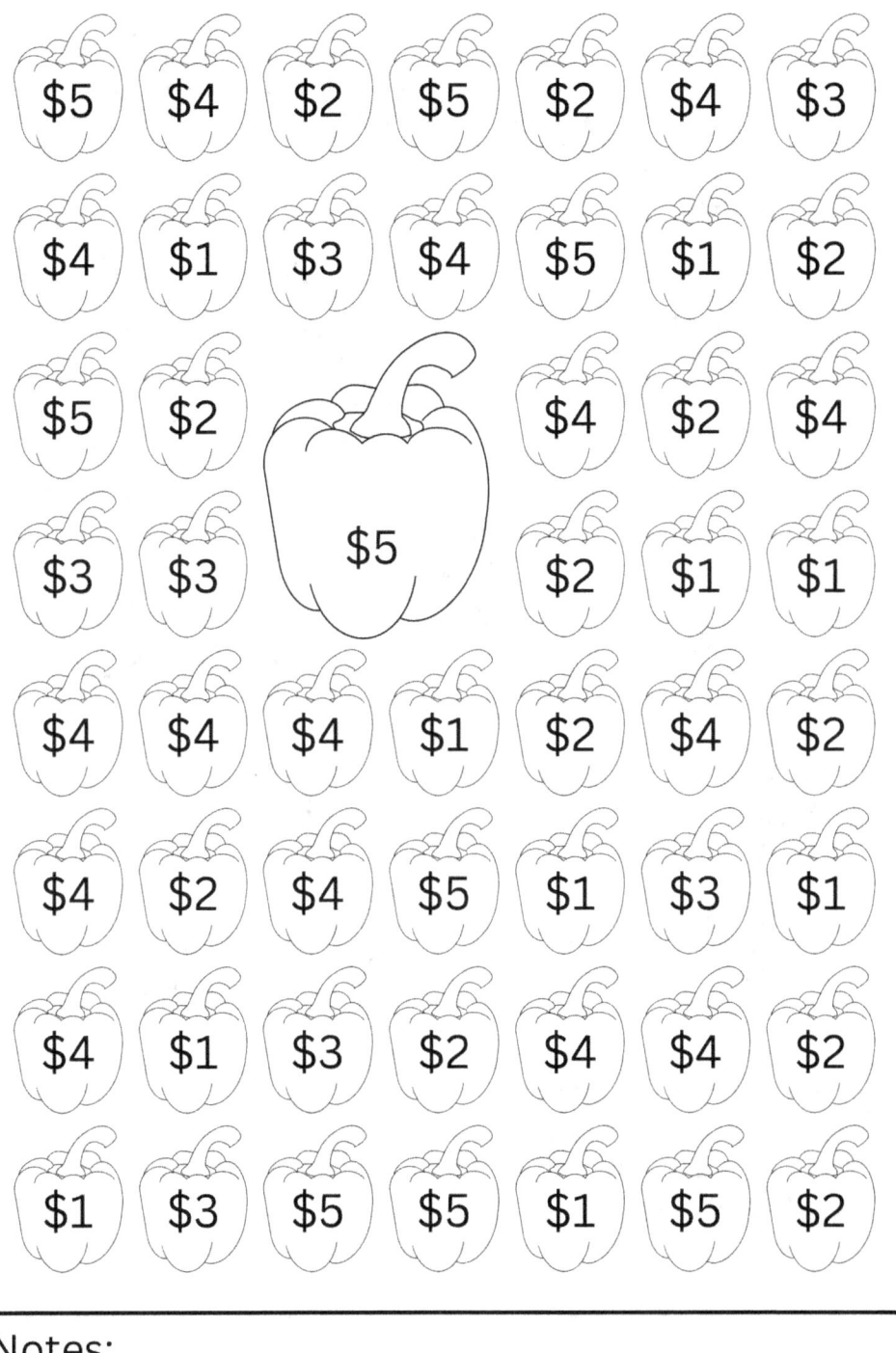

Notes: _____

Let's Save .... $85 in 28 Days

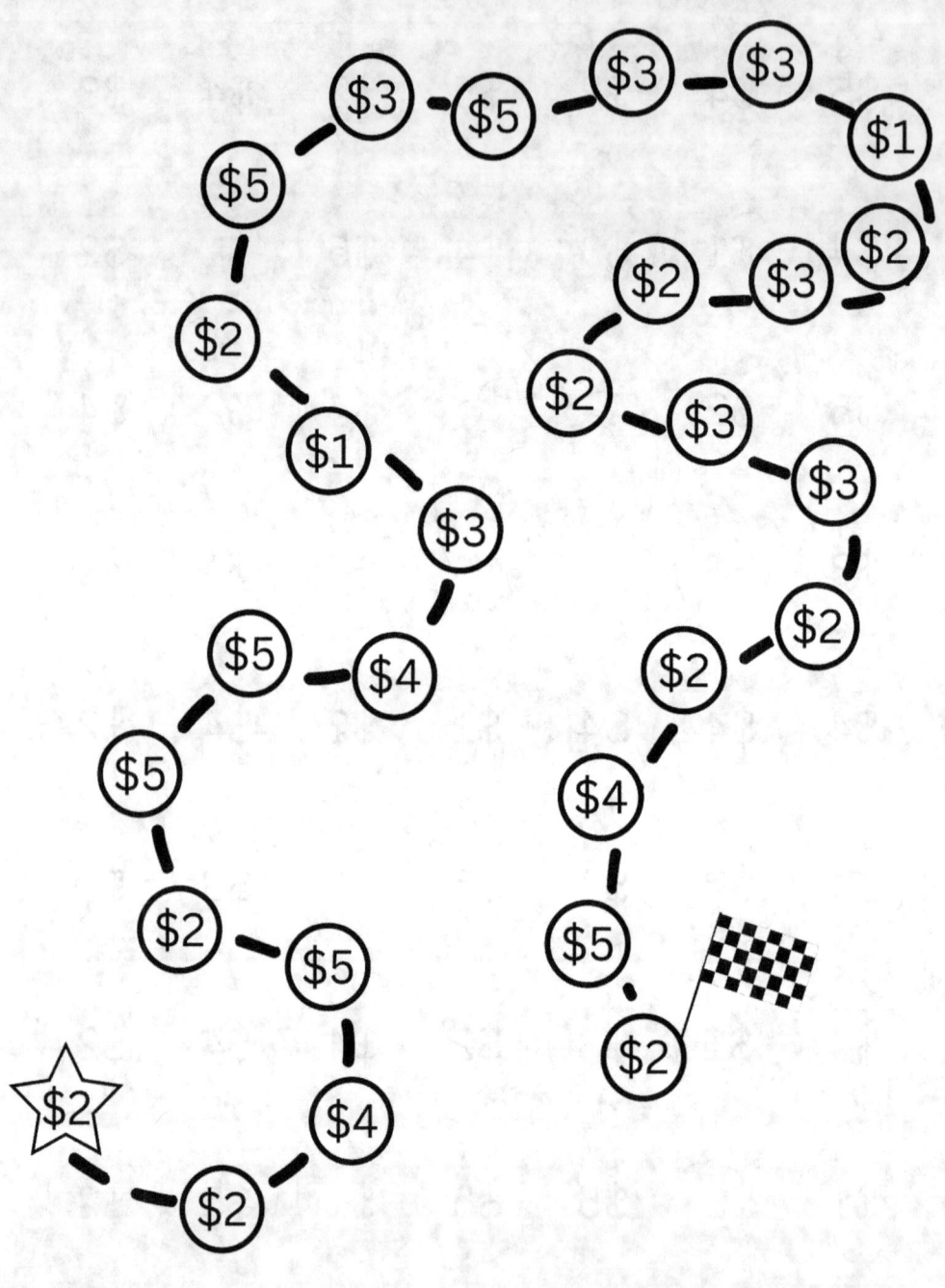

Notes: _____
_____

Let's Save .... $255 in 75 Days

$4		$4	$1	$4			$5	$3	$3
$3		$5		$3	$4	$5	$3		$3
$1	$4	$1							$5
				$4	$2	$3	$1	$4	$3
$2	$2	$5	$5	$2					
$3						$3	$5	$4	$5
$4	$5	$2	$5	$2	$3	$4			$5
									$2
$1	$4	$1	$5	$1		$1	$5	$5	
$3				$2		$3			
$1				$4	$4	$5	$2		
$4									$4
$3		$4	$5	$4	$3				$5
$4	$1	$5			$5	$5	$5	$3	$2

Notes: _____
_____

Let's Save .... $105 in 33 Days

Notes: _____

Let's Save .... $160 in 51 Days

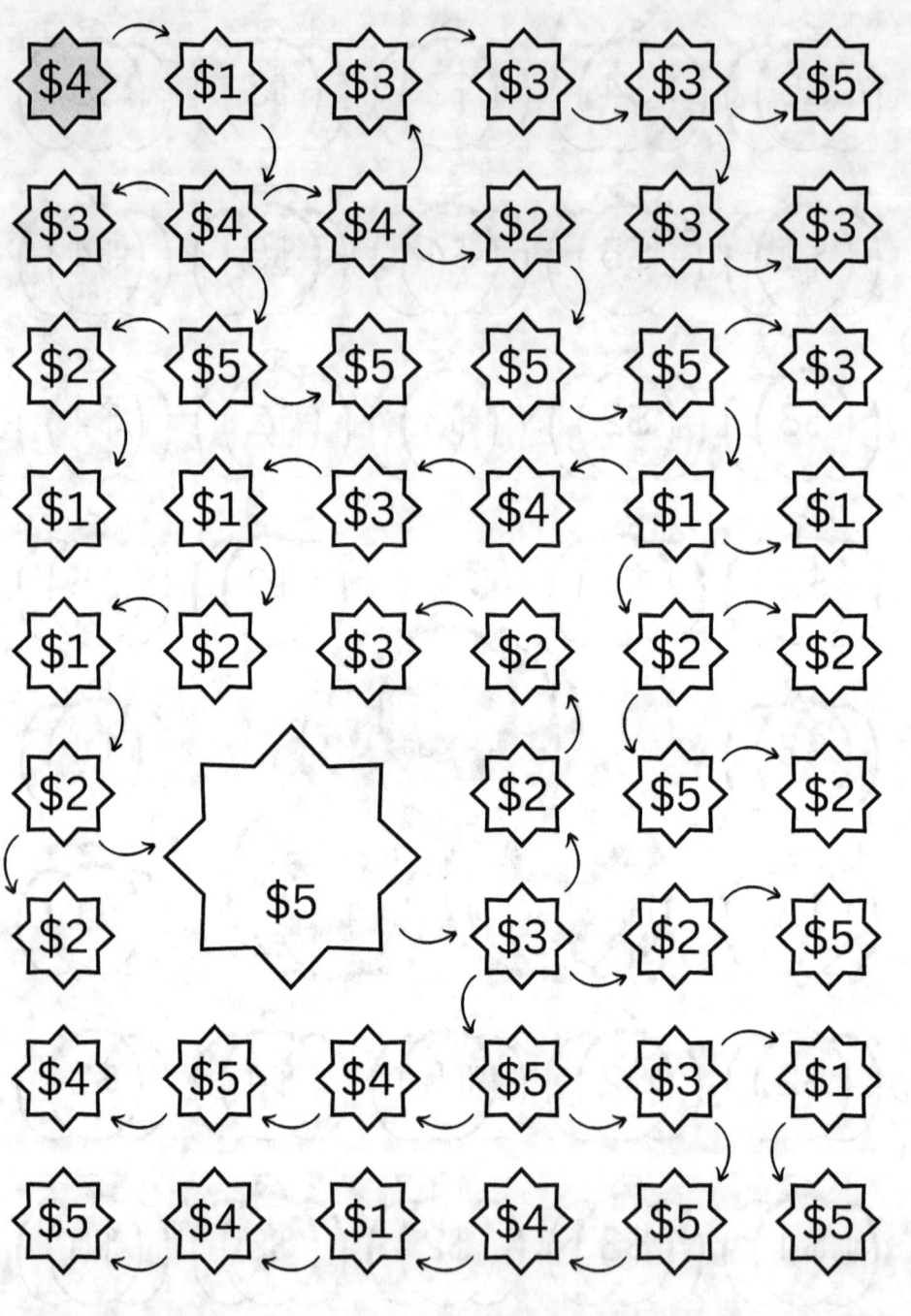

Notes: _____

Let's Save .... $115 in 39 Days

Notes: _____
_____

Let's Save .... $135 in 45 Days

$2 → $3 → $4 → $1 → $3
                          ↓
$2 $3 ← $3 ← $4 $5
↑   ↓   ↑
$4 ← $3 $5 → $1 $2
↓   ↑   ↓   ↑
$1 $2 ← $3 $5 → $4
↓   ↑   ↓
$2 → $3 $2 ← $1 $3
↓   ↑   ↓
$5 $2 → $5 → $2 $2
↓   ↑   ↓
$3 $3 ← $1 ← $4 ← $5
↓
$4 $4 ← $2 ← $3 → $3
↓   ↑   ↓
$4 → $2 → $4 → $4 $2

Notes: _____

Let's Save .... $155 in 48 Days

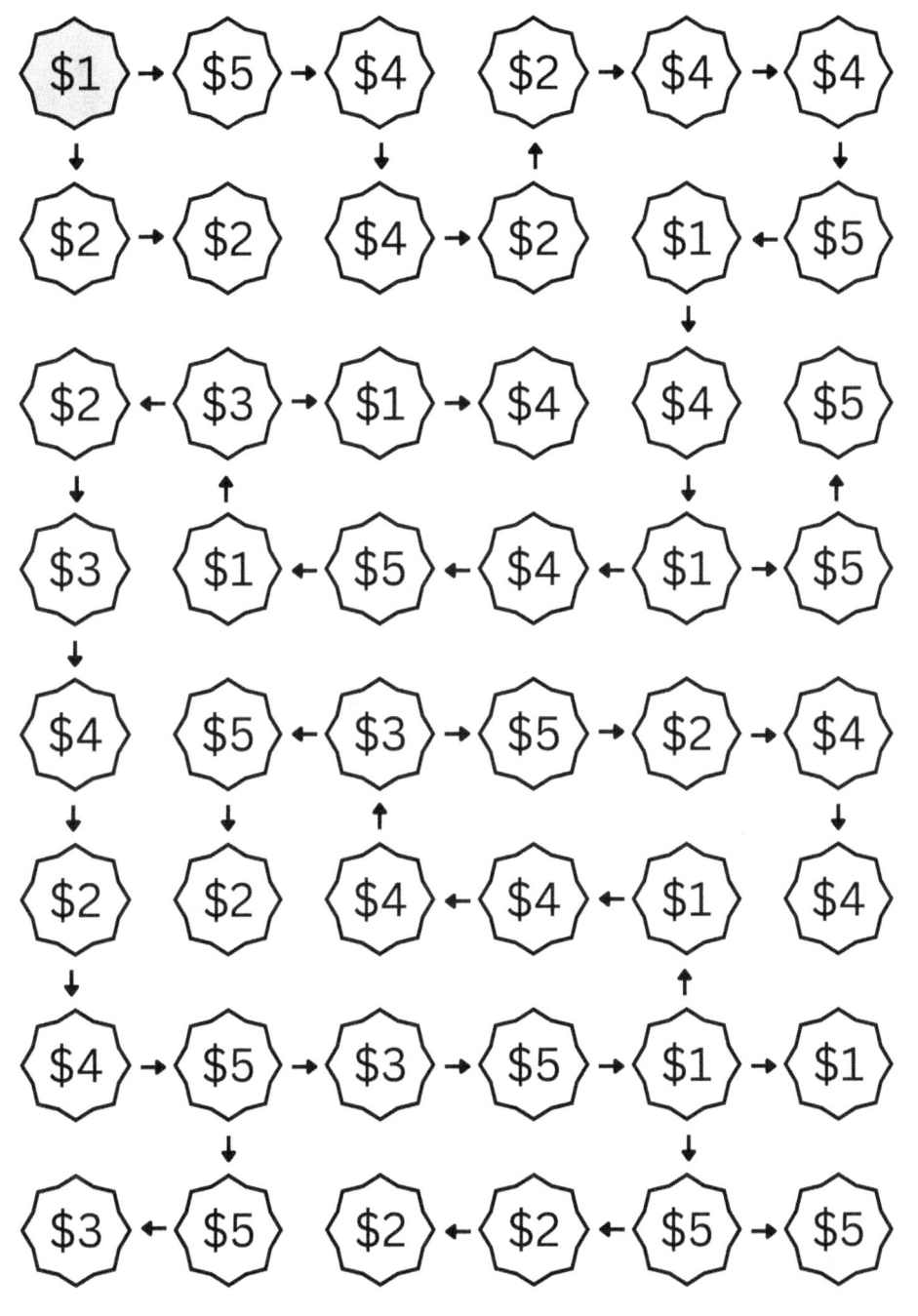

Notes: _____

Let's Save .... $85 in 29 Days

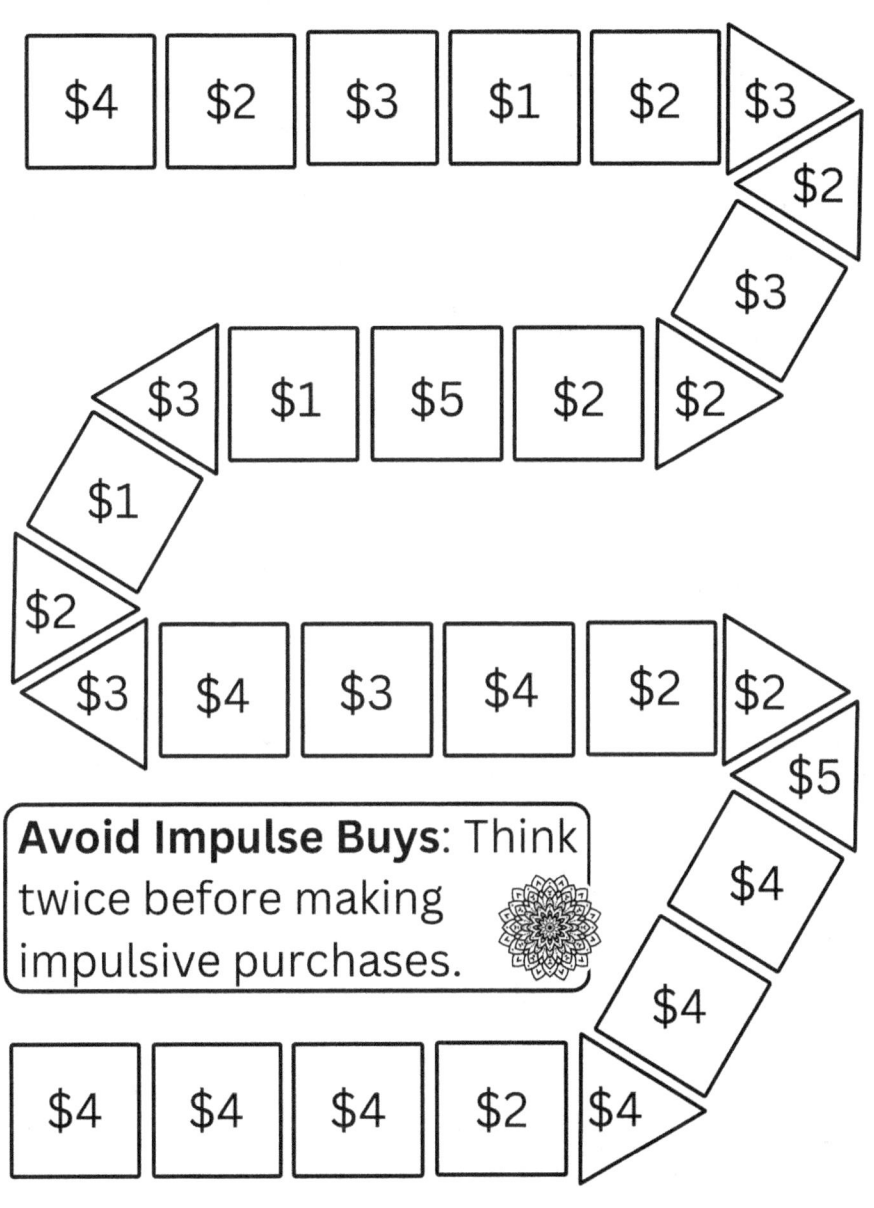

Notes: _____
_____

Let's Save .... $95 in 29 Days

Notes: _____
_____

Let's Save .... $275 in 85 Days

$3	$1
$4	$3

$3	$3
$5	$3
$4	$5

$3

		$2	$4
		$3	$3

$2	$5	$5	$5	$1

$1	$4	$3	$5
$1	$2	$5	$2

$3	$3	$3
$1	$4	$1
$1	$4	$3
$2	$5	$5

$3

$3	$1
$4	$5

$2	$5	$5
$1	$2	$1
$2	$4	$5

$5	$5
$5	$1
$5	$5
$2	$5

$3	$1
$5	$2
$3	$5

$1

$2	$3
$1	$5

$5	$4	$3	$4
$2	$5	$1	$5
$1	$3	$5	$5

Notes: _____
_____

Let's Save .... $465 in 143 Days

Notes: _____

Let's Save .... $260 in 83 Days

Notes: _____
_____

Let's Save .... $165 in 54 Days

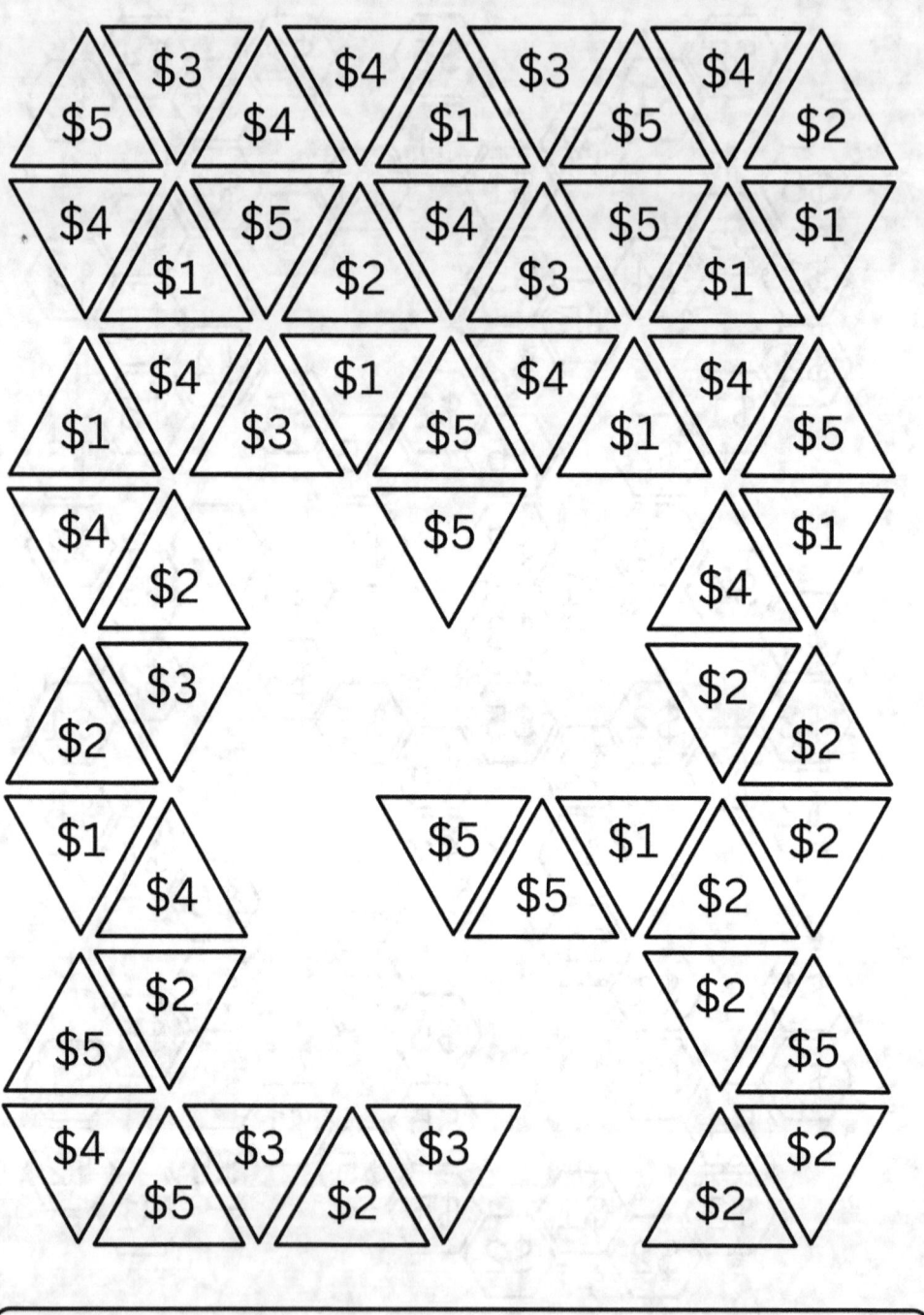

Notes: _____
_____

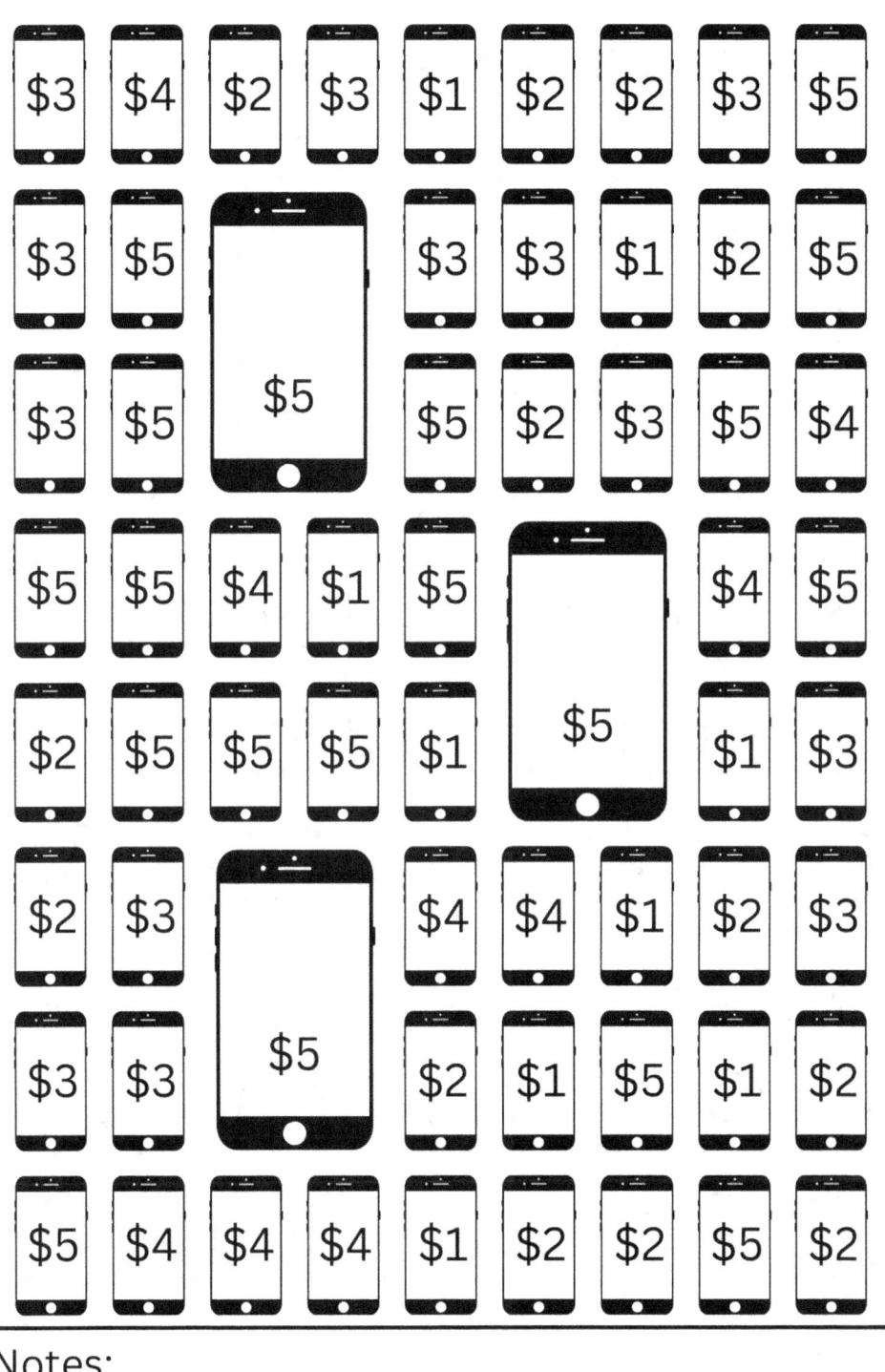

Let's Save .... $205 in 63 Days

Notes: _____

Let's Save .... $225 in 74 Days

$1	$5	$2	$5	$1	$4	$1	$3
$5	$5	$2	$1	$3	$5	$3	$2
$3	$3	$5	$5	$5		$3	$2
$1	$5	$1	$5			$4	$1
$2	$1	$5	$5	$1	$1	$3	$1
$1	$1	$4	$1	$5	$5	$2	$3
$5	$2			$3	$4	$1	$5
$4	$4		$1	$4	$4	$3	$1
$3	$4	$2	$3	$3	$1	$5	$1
$5	$4	$2	$6	$1	$5	$5	$2

Notes: _____
_____

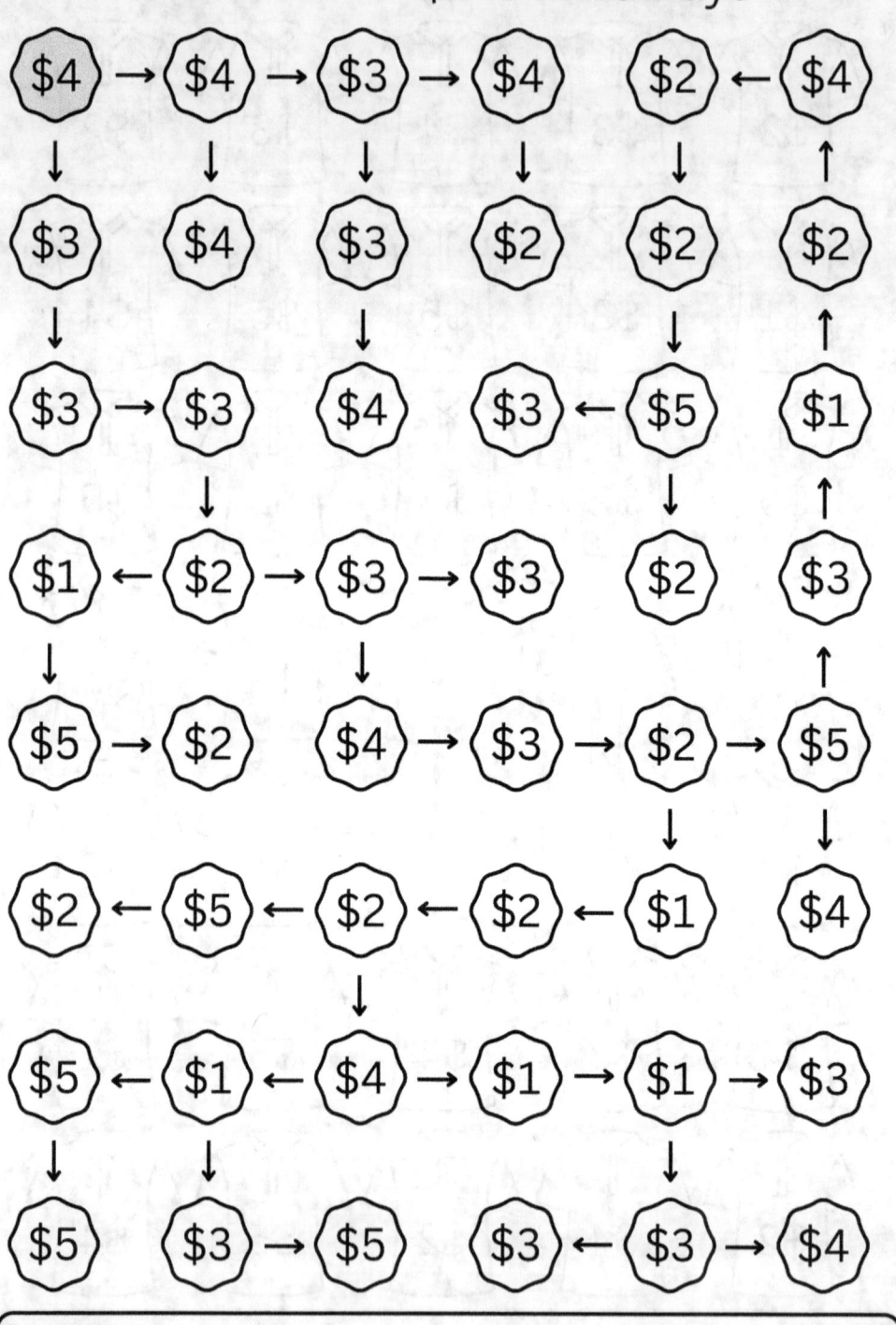

Let's Save .... $95 in 30 Days

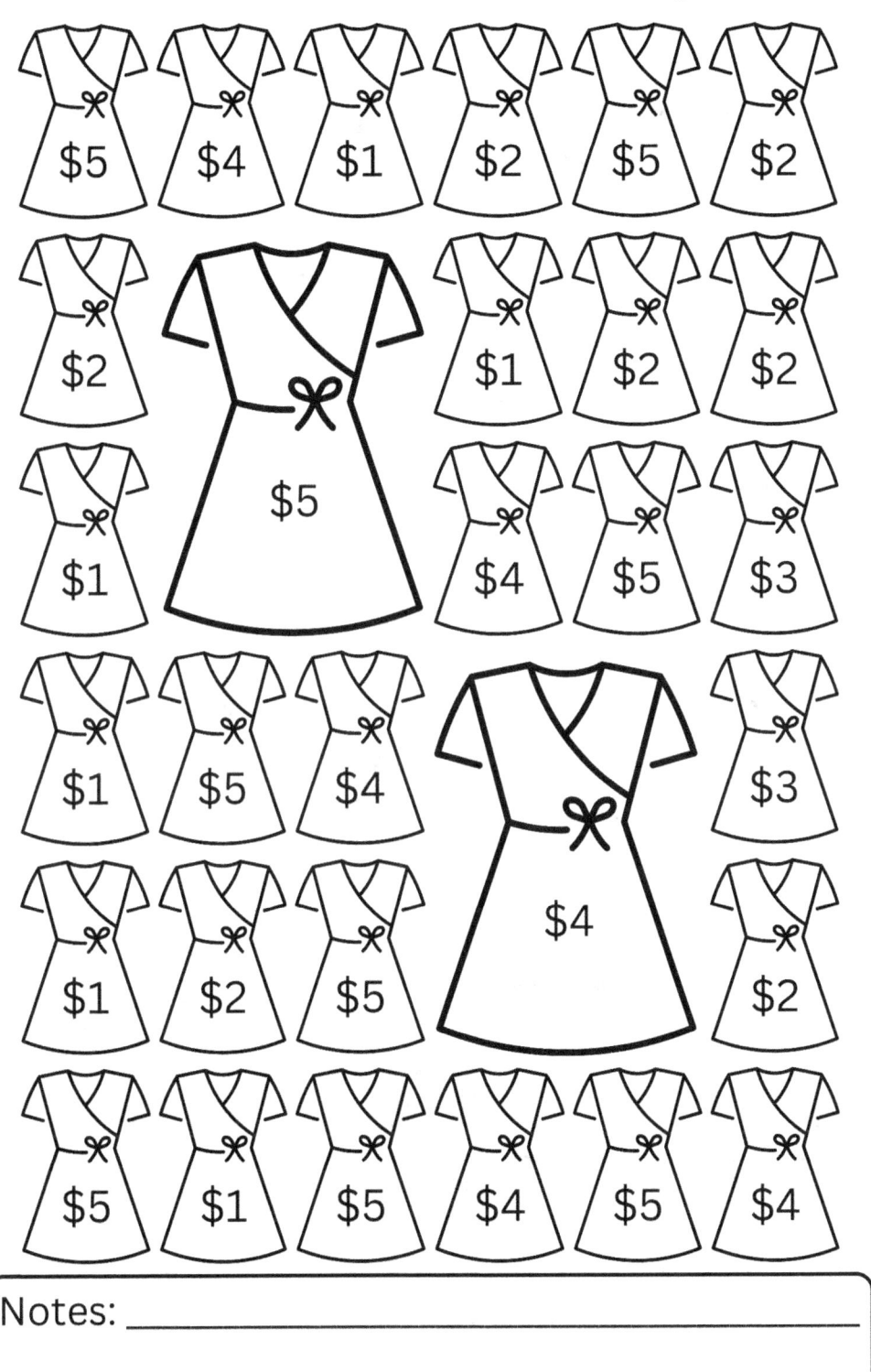

Notes: _____

Let's Save .... $45 in 15 Days

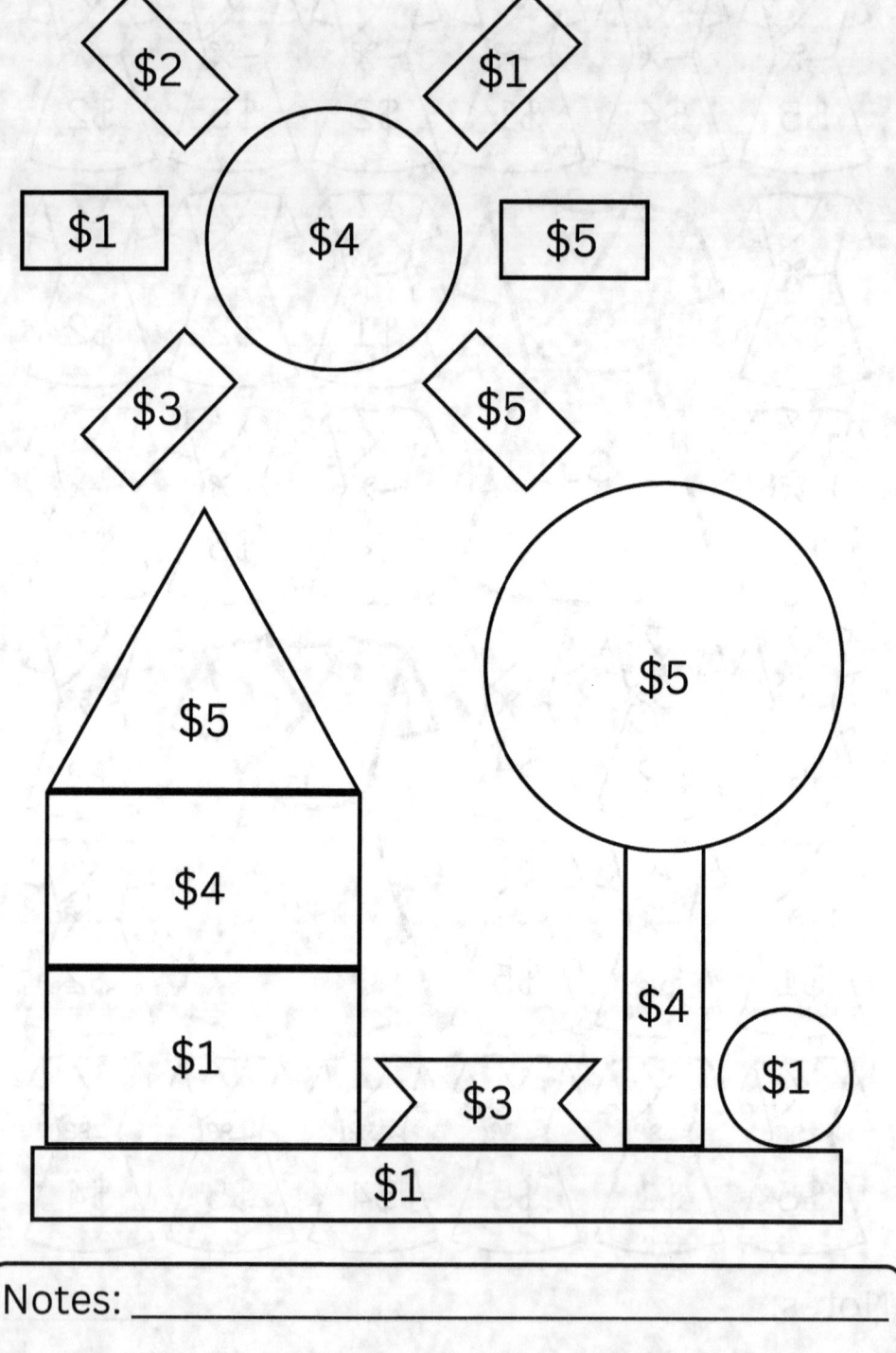

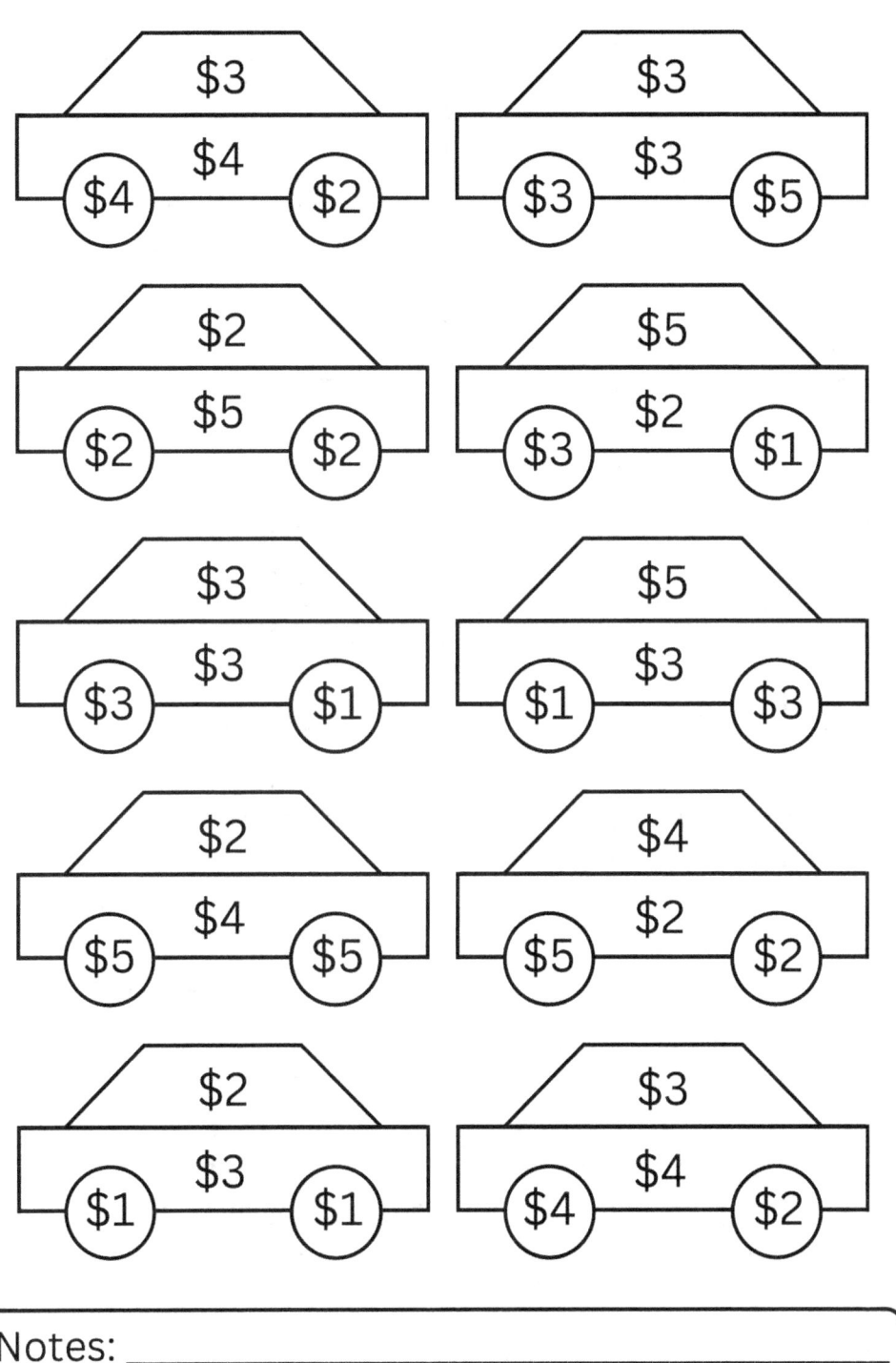

Let's Save .... $245 in 81 Days

Let's Save .... $145 in 48 Days

Notes: _____
_____

Let's Save .... $175 in 53 Days

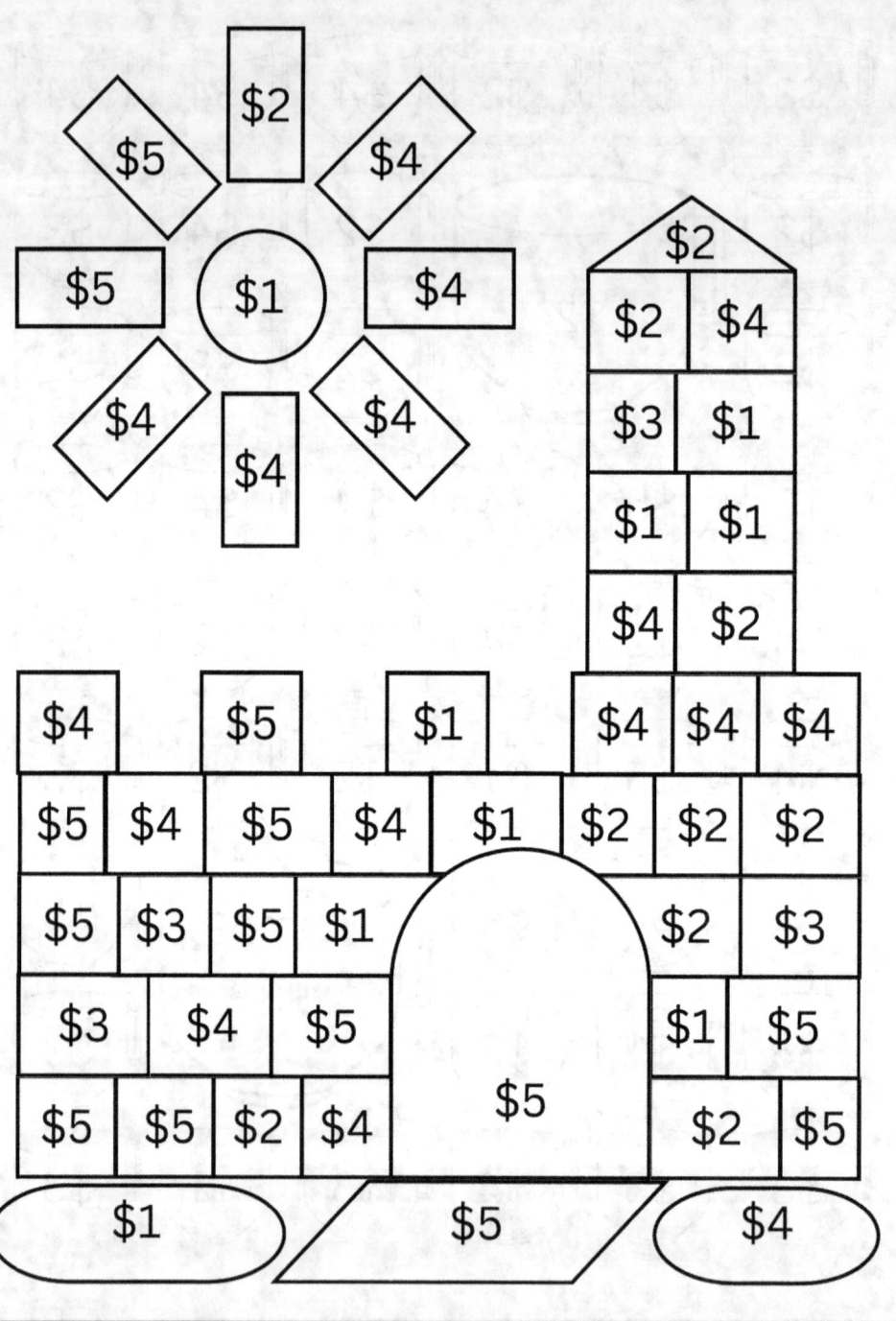

Notes: _____

Let's Save .... $70 in 21 Days

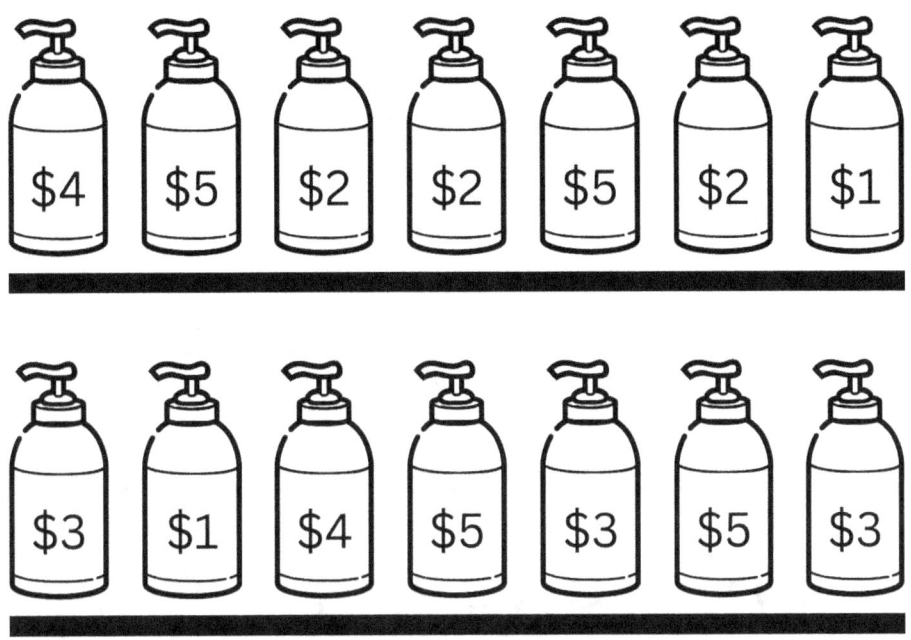

 **Use a Piggy Bank**: Use a piggy bank or clear jar to visualize your savings.

Notes: _____
_____

Let's Save .... $165 in 53 Days

Notes: _____
_____

Let's Save .... $85 in 24 Days

Save Your Allowance: Save your weekly allowance to build savings habits.

Notes: _____

Let's Save .... $125 in 40 Days

ICE CREAMS

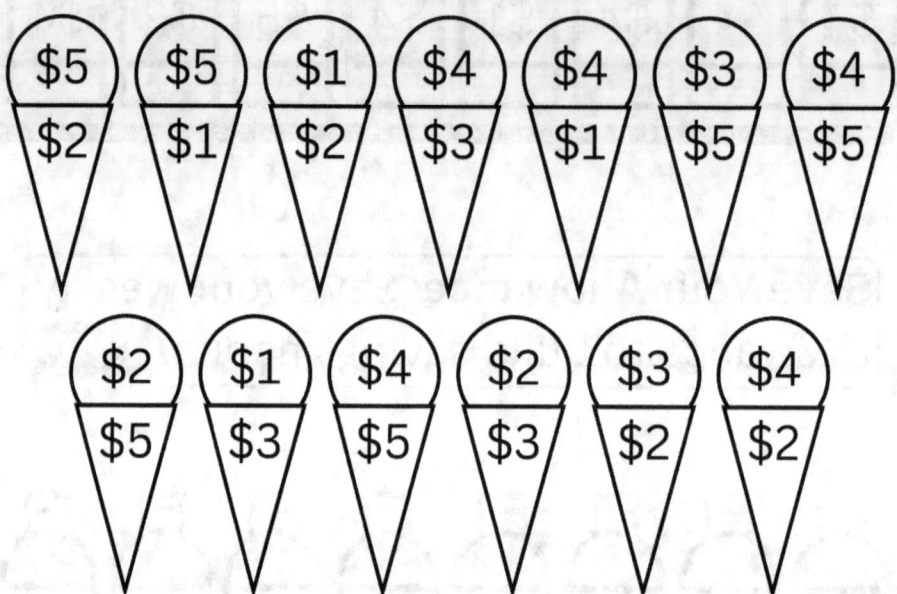

| $5 | $5 | $1 | $4 | $4 | $3 | $4 |
| $2 | $1 | $2 | $3 | $1 | $5 | $5 |

| $2 | $1 | $4 | $2 | $3 | $4 |
| $5 | $3 | $5 | $3 | $2 | $2 |

Save Your Change: Save your loose change to build your savings over time.

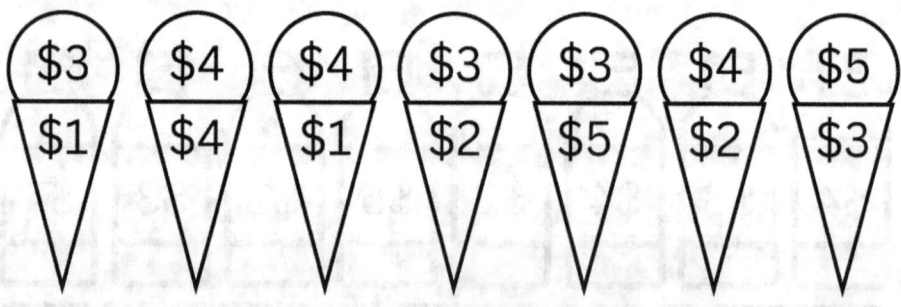

| $3 | $4 | $4 | $3 | $3 | $4 | $5 |
| $1 | $4 | $1 | $2 | $5 | $2 | $3 |

Notes: _____
_____

Let's Save .... $145 in 44 Days

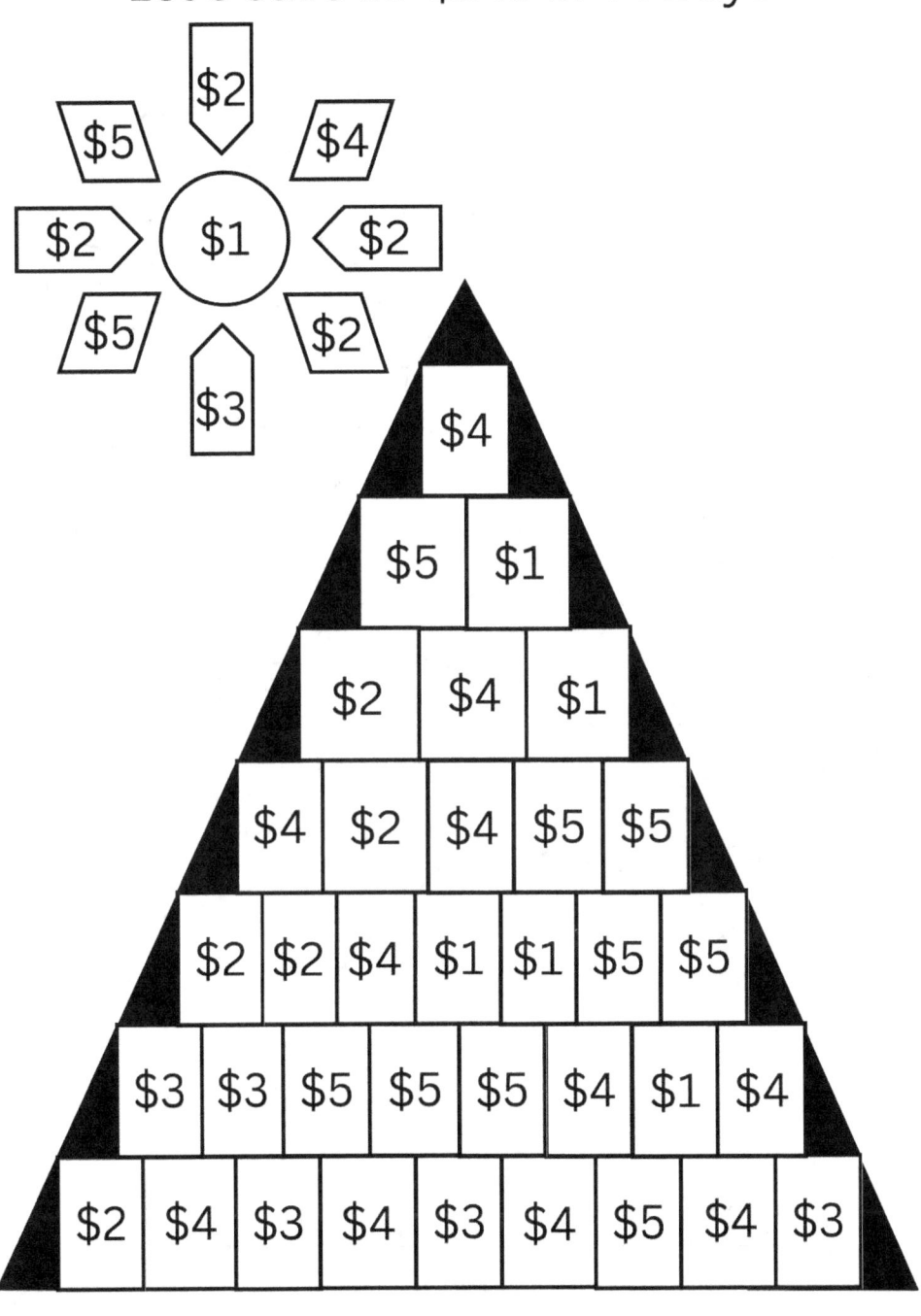

Notes: _____

Let's Save .... $70 in 24 Days

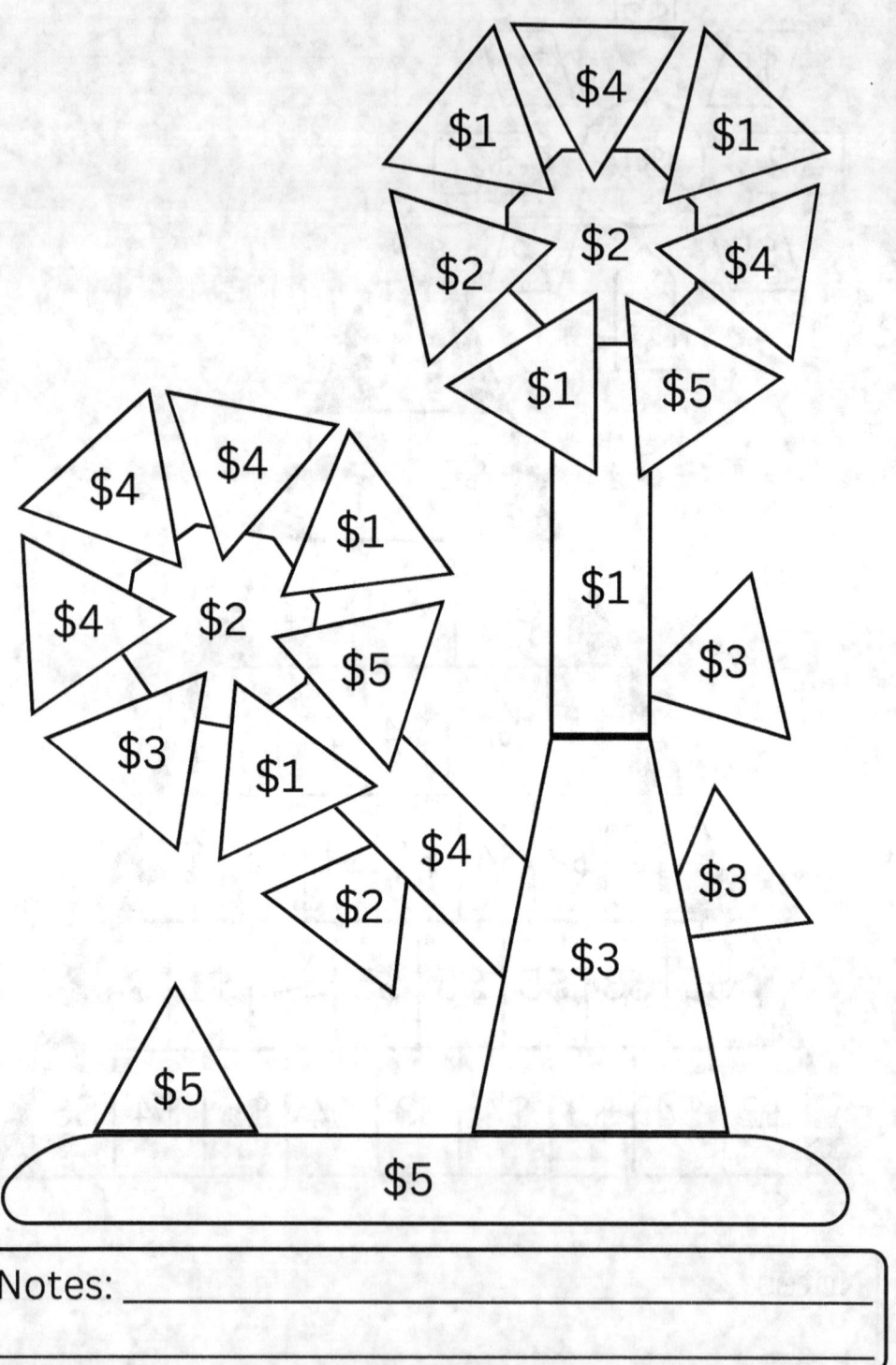

Notes: _____
_____

Let's Save .... $120 in 35 Days

Notes: _____
_____

Let's Save .... $75 in 24 Days

Notes: _____

Let's Save .... $85 in 24 Days

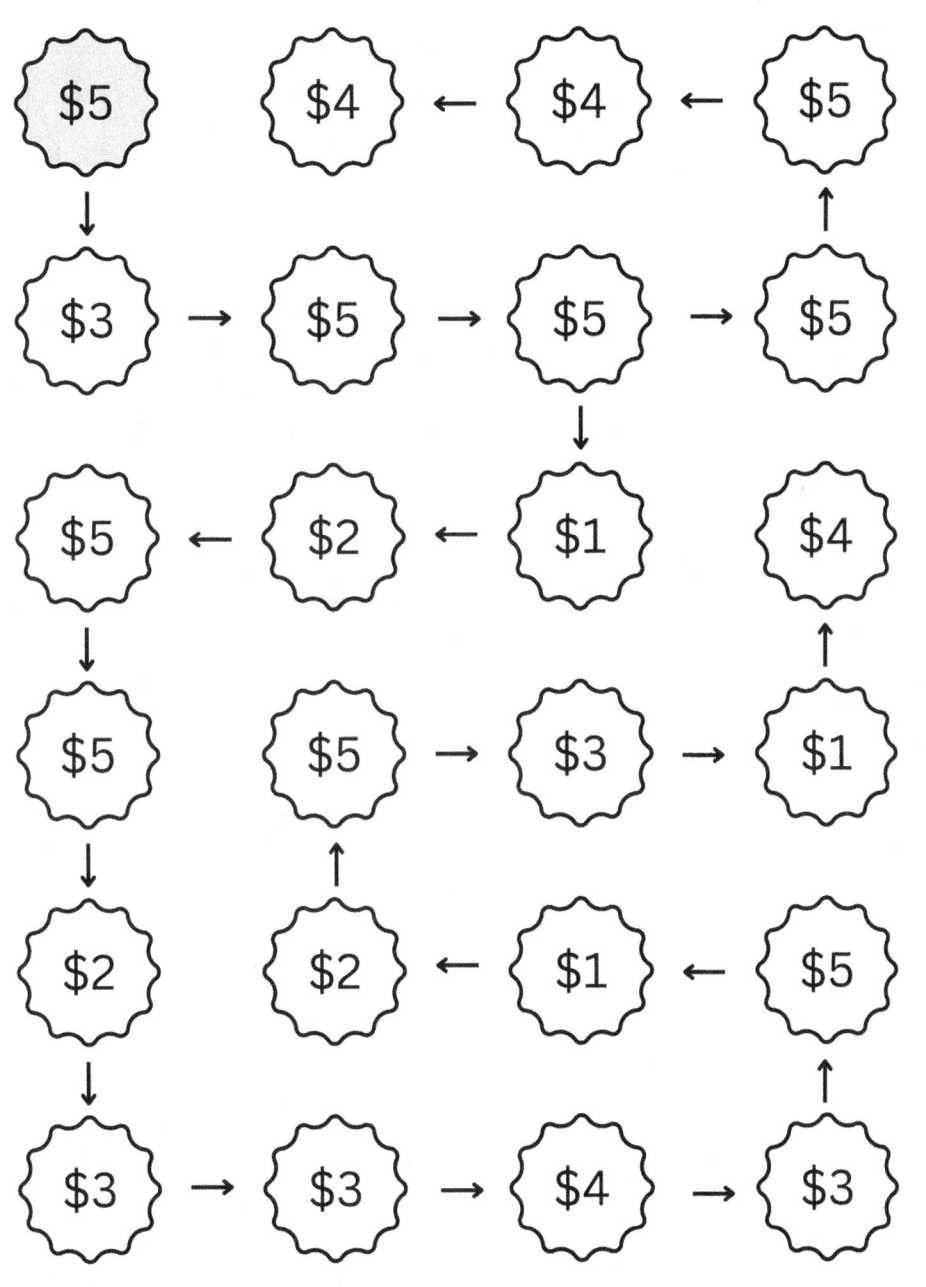

Notes: _____

Let's Save .... $75 in 24 Days

Notes: _____
_____

www.ingramcontent.com/pod-product-compliance
Lightning Source LLC
Chambersburg PA
CBHW071836210526
45479CB00001B/161